COLLECTOR'S GUIDE TO Porcelier CHINA

D1063100

Susan E. Grindberg

COLLECTOR BOOKS
A Division of Schroeder Publishing Co., Inc.

The current values in this book should be used only as a guide. They are not intended to set prices, which vary from one section of the country to another. Auction prices as well as dealer prices vary greatly and are affected by condition as well as demand. Neither the Author nor the Publisher assumes responsibility for any losses that might be incurred as a result of consulting this guide.

Searching For A Publisher?

We are always looking for knowledgeable people considered to be experts within their fields. If you feel that there is a real need for a book on your collectible subject and have a large comprehensive collection, contact Collector Books.

Photography by Rich Littlefield of St. Paul, MN.

Cover Design: Beth Summers
Book Design: Benjamin R. Faust

ON THE COVER: Pictured on the cover are a 6-cup Nautical pot and ceramic dripper with original label, $40.00 – 50.00; a 5" 1939 New York World's Fair disc pitcher, $125.00 – 150.00; and a Basketweave Wild Flowers toaster, $800.00 – 900.00.

Additional copies of this book may be ordered from:

COLLECTOR BOOKS
P.O. Box 3009
Paducah, KY 42002-3009

@ $18.95. Add $2.00 for postage and handling.

Copyright: Susan E. Grindberg, 1996

Dedication

This book is dedicated to all the men and women who worked at Porcelier throughout the years. Without them, these beautiful products could not have been made. I thank them for giving so much enjoyment to me and others.

Acknowledgments

First and foremost, I would like to thank my husband Chuck, for his continued support in this project and for letting me buy and display (everywhere in our home) each and every piece of Porcelier that "I just couldn't live without."

Secondly, I need to thank my good friend, Rich Littlefield, for a crash course in Photography 101 and the use of all his equipment while I was traveling the country taking pictures when he could not go. I also want to thank him for his patience when I put him through grueling photo sessions for the majority of the pictures contained in this book.

Next I would like to thank all of the collectors and dealers who shared information and allowed me to take pictures of their pieces for this book. Some of them put me up for a few days and let me take over their houses with all of the needed equipment, while others trusted me to take boxes of Porcelier to my house or hotel to photograph and return later. They are: Jim Barker, Don Brewer, Dave Carlson, Cindy Fahr, Dave and Betty Gustafson, Steve Gustafson, Chris and Shirley Hall, John and Nancy Hedrick, Lois Lehner, Kathryn McGrew-Payne, Barry Moe, Kevin Nolan, Anthony and Nancy Pushnik, Greg and Chris Seidenberger, Frank Simonie, Gary and Myrna Stewart, Kevin and Marilyn Stein, and Barb Stussy.

I also want to thank all the dealers and collectors from around the country who assisted me with the pricing. There is not enough room to mention them all. It truly was appreciated.

Finally, my most sincere thanks to all the past employees and relatives of past employees for interviews, photographs of their pieces, and copies of old photographs and brochures from the days of Porcelier. Without them, a lot of this information would be lost. They are: Pauline (Kobler) Almquist, Dorothy (Long) Anderson, Austin and Mary (Davis) Book, Joe and Mildred (Harold) Cochran, Virginia (Keys) Dira, Bill and Janet (Downs) Dorey, Vera Downs (widow of Bill Downs), Edith (Downs) Dunn, Ruth Elliott, Francis Erwin, Ann (Lazor) Fadrosh, Virginia (Elliott) Fancsalsky, Jane Giron, Al and Betty Ann (Schlotter) Goodlin, Margaret (Tossie) Hasenstab, Emily (Quatse) Just, Susan (Cepullio) Karfelt, Rose (Pastor) Kintigh, Marian Kleiner, Elizabeth Lazor, John Lewis (grandson of Mae Lewis), Margaret (Leech) Little, Ben Long and Pat (Long) Price (children of Carl Long), Roland and Eunice Long, William and Agnes Long, Anita McIlvaine (daughter-in-law of Ellen McIlvaine), Carol (Kobler) McLaughlin, Freda (Bickel) Morris, Helen (Parise) Palmieri, Jenny (Gillio) Perotti, Betty Quatse, Ilene Reagan-Auen (daughter of George Reagan), Angie Sassos (daughter-in-law of Nick Sassos), Mildred Sivak (widow of Stephen Sivak), Pat Sivak (daughter of Stephen Sivak), Family of Frank Stouffer, Sue Wassil, Erin Weaver (daughter of Ellen McIlvaine), and Betty (Kelly) Yothers.

If I have left anyone out, it was not intentional, and please accept my deepest appreciation and apology.

Contents

Contents, continued. . .

Preface

This book will relate what is known about the Porcelier Manufacturing Co. and the items that they made. It is centered around the kitchenware and light fixture lines produced first in East Liverpool, OH, and then in Greensburg, PA. I have not intentionally omitted any product lines and do not wish to offend anyone whose favorite item(s) are not pictured herein.

Pricing

Values in this book are intended only as a guide. They should not be used to set prices, which may vary from one part of the country to another. I have estimated the values using information obtained from dealers and collectors across the country and have tried to reflect the average price per piece in consideration of regional economic differences and availability.

The values assume that the pieces are in mint condition. They do not include drippers, unless specified. Add $3.00 – 5.00 for a metal dripper without a label; $5.00 – 10.00 for a plain ceramic dripper without a label; and $10.00 – 20.00 for either dripper with an original label intact. UND designates an undetermined value.

I wish to express my thanks to Jim Barker for his expertise and assistance with the valuations on the electrical pieces in the Matched Appliance Sets section of this book.

About the Author

Sue Grindberg lives in Inver Grove Heights, Minnesota, with her family. She is an avid collector of Porcelier China and welcomes the chance to correspond with other collectors. If you write and require a response, you must enclose a self-addressed stamped envelope. Sue Grindberg, 6330 Doffing Ave. E., Inver Grove Heights, MN 55076.

Introduction

I bought my first Porcelier in 1992. It was a two-cup pot in the Country Life design. It did not have a lid and I called it Cottage. I bought it because it had a border of little hearts around the rim and my last name at the time was Hart. When I discovered the Nautical and Dutch Boy and Girl pots, the hunt was on.

In my search for more, I also began to look for information about the Porcelier Manufacturing Company. I bought all the reference books on china and dinnerware to no avail. When I discovered *Lehner's Encyclopedia of U.S. Marks*, I thought I had struck it rich. Unfortunately, the only other information available at the time was Mrs. Lehner's few paragraphs in her *American Kitchen and Dinner Wares* book.

Because of my love of Porcelier, I truly believed that these wonderful pieces had been unfairly overlooked in all of the antiques and collectibles books. It was then that I decided to write to Mrs. Lehner and see if she could give me any leads on where to begin my research. By that time I had amassed enough pieces that there was no turning back. Mrs. Lehner's positive response and feedback was the catalyst that I needed to seriously pursue a project such as this book. I sincerely wish to thank her for taking the time to answer my letters and to share her prior research with me.

In this book, I have purposely used the generic description pot rather than coffee pot or teapot as they were marketed as both with few exceptions. For example, an ad in a Sears catalog read "Vitrified china coffee maker in ivory color. . . China cover fits both top and bottom parts. May be used as a teapot." Many ads designated them as a coffee pot if there was a dripper included and a teapot if not. Even then, they still pointed out that a coffee pot could be a teapot. Thus, pot seemed to fit both occasions.

The sugar bowls, creamers, two-cup pots, and other accompanying pieces are usually decorated with an abbreviated portion of the coffee pot or electric percolator design. They are not always marked, but the shapes follow the same lines as the pots and can usually be identified as Porcelier with little trouble. Because of their similarity to Hall China, I have found it helpful to learn the Hall patterns to be able to, by process of elimination, confirm a new pattern to be Porcelier. I hope this book will assist others in identification and take most of the guesswork out of their collecting.

As you look through the pictures in this book, please take note that I have intentionally left lids off pots where the correct one was not available. Even as an advanced collector, I will occasionally purchase a pot and get it home before I notice that it has the wrong lid. By only showing the correct lids, I am helping you learn what they are supposed to look like. Some people simply believe that a wrong lid is better than no lid and can't resist putting something on top of a pot. I have even seen a dark brown lid on an ivory pot as if it belonged there! The hardest ones to detect, however, are a Porcelier lid on the wrong Porcelier pot. The color and feel are so right that you may not notice the error right away. By the time you get home, it's too late. Practice the "buyer beware" policy and know what you are buying beforehand. The right lids are hard to find, especially on something specialized such as the Tree Trunk or the 1939 New York World's Fair. I have also left drippers off most pieces and have shown only a couple of the pans for the double boilers as they are pretty standard.

As for the pattern names, some of them are company given, some had only catalog numbers, and others I took the liberty of naming (with help from other collectors). Catalog numbers appear in parentheses behind the item being referred to, when known. In order to discuss a particular piece with another person, it had to be called something. This facilitated both persons in a conversation knowing what the other was talking about. I have reverted back to an official company name, if and when one was verified.

I have listed only items whose existence has been verified through catalogs, brochures, or by seeing actual pieces. Speculation on the existence of other pieces may be mentioned but is clearly stated as such.

Finally, I have tried to organize this book in a logical sequence to make it user friendly. But just when I think it all makes sense, something completely new surfaces and it just doesn't fit into any of my well-planned categories. Be assured that there is a system to the madness — the madness being a ***"Porcelier Passion."***

A Bit of History . . .

Who, What, When, and Where

The history of the Porcelier Manufacturing Company has, been sketchy, at best. It has been addressed only a few times in various publications and the total information related has been a paragraph or two. Unfortunately, there has been little uncovered in the way of company records. Most of this history has been pieced together from copies of documents on file with the State of Pennsylvania, the U.S. Patent Office, sales brochures, catalogs, and discussions with former employees or their family members.

The Porcelier Manufacturing Company began in East Liverpool, OH. The exact date is uncertain but has been previously published as 1927.[1]

The company first applied for incorporation on Sept. 3, 1926, in the City of Pittsburgh, Allegheny County, PA. The incorporation was granted on Oct. 14, 1926. The incorporation documents stated that the company intended to conduct business in Pittsburgh, PA. At the time, the actual production was done in East Liverpool with only a sales office in Pittsburgh.

The corporate directors were listed as Hyman Tauber, Treasurer; Harry M. Tauber, and Jacob Dym, all of Pittsburgh, PA. According to the documents filed, the purpose of the corporation was "buying, selling, assembling, manufacturing and dealing in lighting fixtures and electrical specialties."

At the time of this filing, each of the three directors were issued 10 shares of stock with a par value of $100 per share. This initial corporation was dissolved on Oct. 22, 1929.

In 1930, Porcelier purchased the vacant plant of the American China Company in South Greensburg.[2] This was located on Huff Avenue between the Pennsylvania Railroad tracks and Broad Street.

Looking east up Huff Avenue in South Greensburg, PA, the Porcelier Mfg. Co. is the second factory on right. Date unknown.

On May 17, 1930, the company filed new incorporation documents in the City of Greensburg, Westmoreland County, PA. This corporation had corporate directors listed as Hyman Tauber, Treasurer; Harry M. Tauber; Jacob Dym; Emanuel Dym; and George Wasser. The incorporation was granted on May 28, 1930. This corporation was going to conduct business in Greensburg, PA.

The second corporation, seemingly was formed to bring in two additional shareholders and to increase the working capital of the company, as it now had 300 shares of $100 par value stock issued. The purpose of incorporation was "manufacturing, buying, selling, decorating, and dealing in porcelain, tile, china, glass, brick, metal, and like substances, and all articles consisting in whole or in part of porcelain, tile, china, glass, brick, metal or any like substance."

Throughout the years, other documents were filed which dealt with increases, changes, and conversions of capital stock. By 1932 there were 12 stockholders in the corporation. Hyman Tauber had become president while George Wasser was the secretary-treasurer of the corporation.

In the late 1930s Porcelier became unionized. They joined the United Electrical, Radio & Machine Workers of America, Local No. 606. This union was affiliated with the CIO. They remained a union shop until their closing in 1954.

On March 19, 1954, Porcelier sold its building and seven acres of land to Pittsburgh Plate Glass Industries of Pittsburgh, PA. As a condition of the sale, they had until July 1, 1954, to vacate the building.[3] Finally on July 8, 1954 the Corporation filed a Certificate of Election to Dissolve. The dissolution was recorded by the Pennsylvania Dept. of State on July 9, 1954, but not officially filed until August 28, 1956, at which time, a Certificate of Dissolution was issued.

The backside of the Porcelier Mfg. Co. in South Greensburg, PA, after a kiln chimney was struck by lightning. Date unknown.

West side of the Porcelier Manufacturing Company in South Greensburg, PA. George Reagan and Austin Book by a rail car of scrap saggers.

Product Lines and Distribution

During the course of its life, Porcelier made over 100 patterns in kitchenware and well over 100 light fixture patterns. The pieces are of such durability that many have survived in mint condition. I have come across many people, including antique dealers, who think that Porcelier is fairly new because the condition and coloring look as if it was "just made yesterday." At the very least, these pieces were made 40 years ago!

The earliest sales catalog uncovered to date puts the company in East Liverpool, OH. It is a lighting fixture catalog and is assumed to be from the late 1920s.

Lighting fixtures began as the main business of Porcelier and remained an active component of the company throughout its existence. Porcelier manufactured every part of the light fixtures with the exception of the glass globes. The globes were purchased mainly from Beaumont Glass of Texas[4] and hand decorated by Porcelier employees when painting was required. They had a machine department that designed and punched the metal pieces on punch presses. The pottery department made all the ceramic parts, right down to the light bulb sockets. They were assembled at the factory and shipped to electrical wholesalers and retailers for sale to the public.

Some past employees believe that Porcelier's market in lighting was hurt by Leviton when it came out with Bakelite and plastic parts for light fixtures. They were cheaper to manufacture and thus could be sold much cheaper than the all-porcelain fixtures. Porcelier had a more difficult time competing in this area.

Porcelier listed in their initial incorporation documents "electrical specialties" as one of the purposes of the incorporation. From my research, I have understood this to mean the electrical kitchen appliances such as the toasters and waffle irons. One former employee proudly told me that "Porcelier was the first company to make all-ceramic electrical appliances." The only catalog I have come across which contains these items is Catalog No. 15 dated 1934. (A special thanks to Jim Barker for providing me with it.) This particular catalog introduces the two largest lines of matched kitchenware that Porcelier made, the Serv-All and Barock-Colonial lines. A copy is included in the Reprints section of this book.

From there, the company branched out into teapots, drip coffee makers, sugar and creamer sets, canisters, and other kitchenware. They also made dinnerware for the Army's National Defense program during World War II.[5]

Their products were sold by in-house salesmen to retailers and catalog sales companies. In *Thomas Register*, December 1940 Edition, Porcelier was listed under lighting fixtures as being in Greensburg, PA, with branch sales offices in Chicago, IL, and New York City, NY. This register of industrial and manufacturing companies also estimated that they had a minimum capital level of over $500,000. Their largest customers were Sears, Roebuck and Co. and Montgomery Wards. This marketing strategy eliminated the need for media advertising aimed at the public. One of the drawbacks was that many items were sold under other company labels such as Sears, Deluxe Sales Co., Heatmaster, Harmony House, and Hankscraft.

Designs

Due to the lack of company records, designers are almost impossible to identify. What little information that follows has been obtained from past employees and the United States Patent Office.

Porcelier employed in-house designers for the most part. On occasion they would employ the services of outside designers, for which a patent was applied. I have included copies of the design drawings from all patents located. They are shown in the Reprints section.

The only in-house designers I could verify are Carl Kobler and the most talented brothers, Emil and Bernhard Hasenstab. The Hasenstab brothers were employed at Porcelier when they were in East Liverpool and came with the company when it moved to Greensburg in 1930.

Sole credit has been given to Emil for the design of the Basketweave Wild Flowers though the brothers worked as a team on many designs. When I had the pleasure of meeting with Emil's widow, she could only attribute this one pattern, positively, as an individual work of Emil's. She recognized many of the other early 1930s patterns but was uncertain which were Emil's and which were Bernhard's designs. These patterns include the Serv-All line, Barock-Colonial, Colonial, Hostess sets, Platinum sets, Double Floral, and the Beehive Floral Spray.

Emil left Porcelier in the late 1930s to go to Shenango China Co., New Castle, PA, and finally returned to East Liverpool, OH, as a designer for Taylor, Smith and Taylor China Co., specializing in dinnerware.

Bernhard left Porcelier a few years later and went to work for Red Wing Potteries in Minnesota then on to several California potteries, specializing in figurines.

Mr. Kobler was employed by Porcelier from the early 1930s until the plant closed in 1954. He has been credited with the designs of Nautical, Dutch Boy and Girl, Mexican, Flight, and the Hearth patterns. He may have designed others, both in the kitchenware and lighting fixture lines. He also is credited with photographing pieces for the company brochures and catalogs.

As for other inventions and designs we have the following various persons contributing to Porcelier products: Thomas W. Beatty of Columbiana, OH; Emanuel Dym of Pittsburgh, PA; Jacob Dym of Pittsburgh, PA; Paul C. Perrin of Pittsburgh, PA; Hyman Tauber of Greensburg, PA; William C. Tregoning of Greensburg, PA; Emil Walder of Greensburg, PA; Chauncey E. Waltman of Chicago, IL; and George Wilson of Greensburg, PA. The Dyms and Mr. Tauber were owners of Porcelier, and it is uncertain whether the other gentlemen were employees or paid outside designers.

Did You Know?

•From an original design there is a block mold made over the sample piece, then a case made over the block mold, then a production mold made from the case. This is done as many times as necessary to produce the number of production molds needed before a single piece is made.

•Porcelier made pieces using the casting, jiggering, and dry press methods.

•Porcelier's tunnel kiln held 39 kiln cars. One car was approximately 6' long by 4' wide by 8' high.

•A filled kiln held between 20,000 and 30,000 pieces of ware.

•It took 39 hours at approximately 2,300° to fire Porcelier's Vitreous China.

•Shrinkage during firing is approximately ⅛th inch to the foot.

•Porcelier used six different clays in their products. 1) Feldspar from North Dakota; 2) Flint from Pennsylvania; 3) #25 English China from England; 4) #88 English China from England; 5) #4 Kentucky Ball from Kentucky; and 6) English Ball from England.

•Porcelier sponsored a men's bowling team.

•Porcelier had an employee credit union.

•Porcelier employees had a fishing club with a clubhouse out in the country.

•Porcelier had an Honor Roll dedicated to employees who served in the armed forces during World War II.

•Porcelier supported the war effort of World War II and spearheaded a scrap metal drive in its parking lot.

•Christmas was celebrated with large departmental parties each year and the company gave employees specially made pieces as gifts in some years.

•Many employees would make unauthorized pieces and paint them special as gifts. Many figurines, ashtrays, and baby plates were made this way. See the Novelty section for more information.

Observations

It is an interesting study to examine the mail-order catalogs through these 30 years and watch the transition of kitchenware evolve from the heavy hand-decorated porcelain coffee maker with ceramic dripper to the porcelain coffee maker with metal dripper to the lighter, more modern all glass or stainless steel coffee makers. At the same time it is sad to watch the sinking of a company as its products dwindle from several styles offered in three or four sizes to two styles (with no choice of style by the customer) then finally to one style in the last years of business. One can just feel the end creeping upon the manufacturer as the retailer is doing its best to deplete his final inventory on hand. It is like watching the end of an era of style and craftsmanship.

As I was visiting past employees it became apparent to me how important Porcelier had been in the lives of most of them. They opened their homes and photo albums to me in an effort to explain how things were and how much of a family the people at Porcelier had been. Many husbands and wives met at Porcelier. Many of them had mothers, fathers, aunts, uncles, and siblings who also worked there. Most had happy memories and were sad and surprised when it closed. A lot would still like to be working at "The Porcelier," as they so fondly call it.

The next few pages are photographs obtained from these wonderful people of the days gone by.

The following five pictures are from various employee social functions. The dates are unknown but they reinforce the feeling of family that most past employees expressed during interviews.

Office staff, Christmas 1943 or 1944.
L to R: Hyman Tauber, William Wolfe, Gertrude Errett, Marg (last name unknown), Florence Jordan, Mariah Baker, Ruth Elliott, Pauline Quartz, Albert Rice, Rosemary McIntyre, Louis Meneghin, Betty Ann Schlotter, David Mundt, and Harry Tauber.

Office staff, Christmas 1944 or 1945.
L to R: Mariah Baker, Mickey Thomas, Gertrude Errett, Shirley Dunn, Albert Rice, Marjorie Lang, Betty Shrader, Florence Jordan, Betty Ann Schlotter, and Ruth Elliott.

Office staff, Christmas, year unknown.

Austin Book, clay department foreman, holding a sagger. A kiln car is constructed of saggers put together in the formation required to hold the pieces being fired at that particular time.

L to R: Frances Long and Bertha Kantar.
Date unknown.

Finishing department, date unknown.
Left to right: Ethel Arnel, Jane Messich, and Mary Sheffler.

Finishing department, late 1940s.
Note Floral Panel percolators in background.

Finishing department, late 1940s – early 1950s.
Note Miniature Rose sugar bowls on shelves.

Finishing department, early to mid 1940s

Clay department, late 1930s – early 1940s.
Posing in front of loaded kiln cars.

Coffee break in the finishing department in the early 1950s.
L to R: unknown and Mae Lewis.

L to R: Joe Schindler, Ed Sturtz, Matt Taylor, John Fowell, and unknown. Date unknown.

Executive Board of the Union, 1942.
Front L to R: Preston Wilkenson, Oscar Koenig, Joseph Zeglin, Edward Harold, and Annie Smith.
Back L to R: Joe Schindler, William Downs, unknown, Fred Ridale, Nick Sassos, and Walter Kloes.

Union Strike of March 1938, outside of Porcelier factory.

The scrap drive spearheaded by Porcelier in the early 1940s for the war effort.

Austin Book with Porcelier's parade float.

Porcelier Manufacturing Company parade entry, late 1930s – early 1940s.

The bowling team, year unknown.
L to R: George Adams, Mr. Altman, Mr. Smith, Emerson Davis, Frank Stouffer, and Mr. Zebalic.

Labels and Marks

Porcelier used a wide variety of marks during their relatively short life. The following photographs show many of the variations used. The first eight are ink stamps. They could be black, blue, brown, or green ink.

The ninth mark was taken from the bottom plate of an electric percolator and the tenth is a paper label from a light fixture. The paper label is green and ivory.

The eleventh is an incised mark from the bottom of a drop-lamp and the twelfth is a raised mark molded into the bottom of an appliance coaster.

They also used foil labels, in gold or silver, on their drippers and examples of them are shown in detail and on the original drippers. I have made a point of showing that Porcelier used both ceramic and metal drippers as I have had many people ask me if the metal ones were replacements. Not necessarily.

No matter which mark was used, it almost always included the words "Porcelier," in script, and "Trade Mark." In addition, it often contained the words "Vitrified China" or "Vitreous China," as this is the type of china Porcelier produced. However, not all pieces were marked. Most of the creamers and sugars bear no mark at all, while identical pots have been found both marked and unmarked.

The last four marks shown are from pieces made by Porcelier for other companies and therefore were marked for the marketing company. Identical pieces have been found to carry the Porcelier name thus tying them to the Porcelier Manufacturing Company.

Besides the four items mentioned above, it has been verified that Porcelier made pieces for Hankscraft. It has been speculated, but not yet verified, that they made Drip-o-lators and some pieces for the Hall China Company. These last items are still being researched. However, it would not be that unusual, as many of the companies of this era placed similar orders with various china makers in order to meet their sales demands.

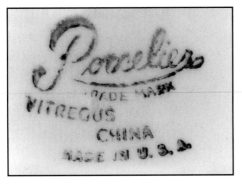

Mark 1

Mark 2

Mark 3

Mark 4

Mark 5

Mark 6

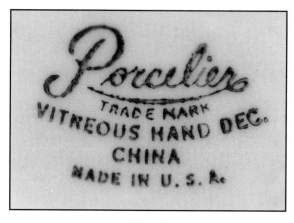

Mark 7

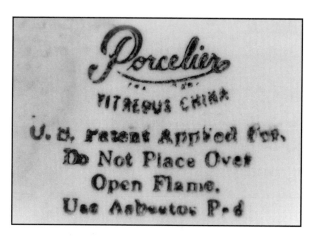

Mark 8

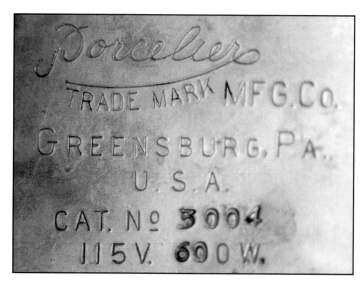

Mark 9
From electric percolator.

Mark 10
From lighting fixture.

Mark 11
From drop lamp.

Mark 12
From appliance coaster.

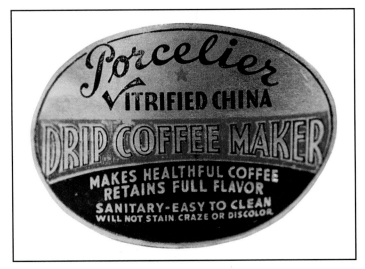

Mark 13
Dripper gold foil label.

Mark 13
Dripper silver foil label.

For comparison of original drippers.

Mark 14
From lighting fixture.

Mark 15
De-luxe Sales Co. mark.

Mark 16
Sears Cattail mark.

Mark 17
Heatmaster mark.

Matched Appliance Sets

This classification includes those sets which have an electrical appliance such as a sandwich grill, toaster, or waffle iron.

All sandwich grills originally came with a grease catcher. It is valued with the Barock-Colonial pattern even though it is interchangable with any pattern.

Basketweave Wild Flowers

This was designed by Emil Hasenstab, an in-house designer, in the mid 1930s. The spaghetti bowl is a special piece which was made to be given to employees as a Christmas gift and was made with several different decals. This set is one of the few patterns that had a decorated dripper that matched the coffee pot. The Wild Flower decal is also used on the Scalloped Wild Flowers set.

The 3-piece percolator set is offered in the 1938 wholesale catalog of the Holsman Company at a cost of $5.25. Another wholesaler, the Paramount Supply Company, had the 3-piece urn set for $5.88, the toaster for $8.57, and your choice of the sandwich grill or the waffle iron for $6.17. This pattern also was seen in the N. Shure Company catalog that same year.

Six-cup pot with a decorated dripper.

Creamer	$12.00
Electric percolator	100.00
Electric urn	130.00
Sandwich grill	225.00 – 275.00
Spaghetti bowl	85.00
Sugar bowl	12.00
Toaster	800.00 – 900.00
Waffle iron	175.00 – 225.00
6-cup pot	45.00
6-cup pot with decorated dripper	75.00

Basketweave Wild Flowers urn, percolator, sugar, and creamer.

Basketweave Wild Flowers sandwich grill and waffle iron.

Basketweave Wild Flowers spaghetti bowl and toaster.

Scalloped Wild Flowers

This pattern also hails from the mid 1930s and has a similar makeup as the Basketweave Wild Flowers. It is suspected that there is an electric urn but I have not yet verified its existence.

Creamer $15.00
Electric percolator 110.00
Sandwich grill . . . . .280.00 – 300.00
Sugar bowl 15.00
Toaster . . . . .900.00 – 1100.00
Waffle iron . . . . .225.00 – 300.00
6-cup pot 45.00

Scalloped Wild Flowers percolator, sugar, and creamer.

Scalloped Wild Flowers 6-cup pot.

Scalloped Wild Flowers toaster.

Scalloped Wild Flowers sandwich grill.

Scalloped Wild Flowers waffle iron.

Barock-Colonial

This larger set was introduced in 1934 along with the Serv-All Line. A copy of the company catalog (including an original wholesale price list) is reprinted in the Reprints section. It has matching light fixtures to "totally coordinate" your kitchen. They are pictured in the Lighting Fixtures section. It was originally offered with gold or red dots and has since been found with blue ones. Note that the decoration in the center of the sandwich grill can be either a pinwheel design (matching the electric percolator) or a floral decal (matching the electric urn). There are 22 pieces in this set.

Collectors often refer to this pattern as Gold Dots, Red Dots, or Blue Dots. Just before completion of this book, a sugar bowl appeared without any color to the decorations. Upon close examination, it does not appear that the color had worn off, it seems that there never was any color to the decoration at all. So there may be other pieces in Ivory Dots.

	Gold	Ivory, Red, or Blue
Batter pitcher (2014)	$40.00	$50.00
Canisters (2016)		
coffee, salt, sugar, and tea (each)	35.00	40.00
Casserole combination (2010) (not shown)	55.00	58.00
Cookie jar (2015)	95.00	105.00
Creamer (2007 or 2009)	12.00	14.00
Electric percolator (2007)	75.00	90.00
Electric urn (2009)	125.00	140.00
Grease catcher (ivory only)		50.00
Pretzel jar	95.00	105.00
Sandwich grill (2004)	200.00 – 275.00	250.00 – 325.00
Shakers (2020)		
flour, pepper, salt, and sugar (each)	15.00	15.00
Sugar bowl (2007 or 2009)	12.00	14.00
Syrup jar (2012)	35.00	45.00
Teapot (2011)	35.00	40.00
Toaster (2002)	800.00 – 900.00	800.00 – 900.00
Waffle iron (461)	150.00 – 225.00	175.00 – 250.00

Barock-Colonial shaker set in gold.

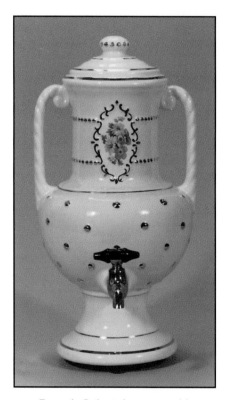

Barock-Colonial urn in gold.

Barock-Colonial teapot in gold.

Barock-Colonial percolator, sugar, and creamer in blue.

Barock-Colonial canister set and cookie jar in gold.

Barock-Colonial pretzel jar in gold.

Barock-Colonial batter pitcher, waffle iron, and syrup jar in gold.

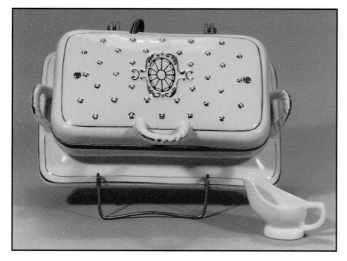

Barock-Colonial sandwich grill and grease catcher in gold.

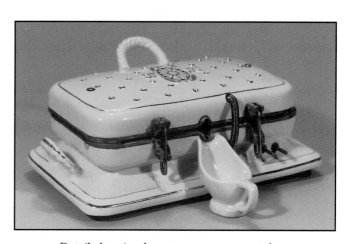

Detail showing how to use grease catcher.

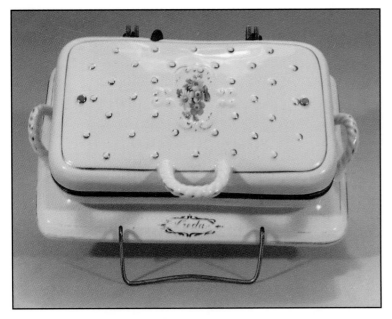

Barock-Colonial sandwich grill with floral decal and personalized "Freda."

Barock-Colonial toaster in blue.

Close-up of toaster controls.

Barock-Colonial percolator, sugar, and creamer in red.
Photo courtesy of Frank Simonie.

Barock-Colonial sugar bowl in solid ivory.

BAROCK – COLONIAL
Created by
PORCELIER MGF CO.–GREENSBURG PA.

Water color painting done by Carl Kobler.
Photo courtesy of Carol (Kobler) McLaughlin.

The Serv-All Line

This line was introduced in a 1934 company sales catalog. It is reprinted in the Reprints section of this book. It is one of the largest kitchen and appliance sets that the company produced. This set also contains 22 pieces and it was originally offered in a choice of platinum, or a red and black color combination. Some pieces in gold have shown up even though they were not an original color choice. It is not clear when they were added as a color option. Note that the platinum- and gold-decorated pieces have an ivory body to them while the red and black decorated pieces are very white.

The sandwich grill and waffle iron have been found with either the Porcelier or Heatmaster marks. See Labels and Marks for more information.

	Platinum	Gold or Red/Black
Batter pitcher (3014)	$35.00	$40.00
Canisters (3016)		
coffee, salt, sugar, and tea (each)	35.00	40.00
Casserole combination (3010) (not shown)	55.00	58.00
Coffee pot (576-D)	35.00	35.00
Cookie jar (3015)	75.00	85.00
Creamer (3007 or 3009)	12.00	12.00
Electric percolator (3007)	90.00	100.00
Electric urn (3009)	110.00	120.00
Pretzel jar	75.00	85.00
Sandwich grill (3004)	150.00 – 225.00	175.00 – 250.00
Shakers (3020) (not shown)		
flour, pepper, salt, and sugar (each)	15.00	15.00
Sugar bowl (3007 or 3009)	12.00	12.00
Syrup jar (3012) (not shown)	30.00	35.00
Teapot (3011)	35.00	35.00
Toaster (3002)	800.00 – 950.00	800.00 – 1,000.00
Waffle iron (451)	100.00 – 150.00	125.00 – 175.00

Serv-All canister set and pretzel jar in platinum.

Serv-All cookie jar in platinum.

Serv-All percolator, sugar, and creamer in platinum.

Serv-All percolator, sugar, and creamer in red and black.

Serv-All percolator, sugar, and creamer in gold.

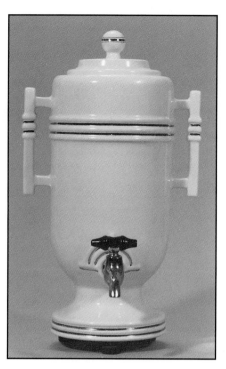

Serv-All urn in platinum.

Serv-All coffee pot in gold.

Serv-All teapot and coffee pot in platinum.

Serv-All toaster in platinum.

Serv-All sandwich grill and grease catcher in platinum. (See Barock-Colonial pattern for grease catcher pricing.)

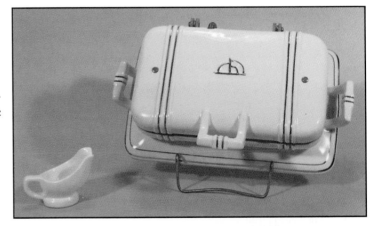

Serv-All waffle iron and batter pitcher in platinum.

Colonial

I am using Colonial to specify the shape rather than the decoration of these pieces. This shape was made in an undecorated ivory, with various Silhouette decals or with a Black-eyed Susan decal. Porcelier also made a small advertising piece which matches this pattern. It is pictured in the Miscellaneous section.

In order to keep track of the silhouette decals, I have named them. They are Bouquet, Introduction, Refusal, Proposal, Acceptance, Minuet, and Piano Lesson. Proposal and Minuet are not shown but depict the man proposing on bended knee and a couple in a minuet stance.

There are more Black-eyed Susan and Silhouette pieces listed in the Hostess, Platinum, and Percolator Sets section.

Undecorated:
4-cup pot $30.00
6-cup pot 35.00
6-cup double pot 65.00

Black-eyed Susan:
6-cup pot 45.00
6-cup double pot 75.00

Silhouette:
Waffle iron . . . . .185.00 – 225.00
6-cup pot 45.00
6-cup double pot 75.00

Colonial undecorated 4-cup pot, undecorated 6-cup double pot, and 6-cup pot with the Introduction decal.

Colonial Silhouette 6-cup double pot; Bouquet decal, top; Introduction decal, bottom.

Colonial Black-eyed Susan 6-cup double pot.

Colonial Silhouette waffle iron, Introduction decal.

Colonial Silhouette waffle iron, Piano Lesson decal.

The Silhouette Decals

Acceptance

Bouquet

Introduction

Close-ups of Refusal, Piano Lesson, Proposal, and Minuet were not available. However, some do appear on pictured items in the Silhouette patterns.

Hostess, Platinum, and Percolator Sets

Included in this section are sets that have at least an electric percolator or urn but no other appliances. They may also have coffee pots and teapots or other accessory pieces.

The graceful heart-shaped sets consisted of either an electric percolator, creamer, and sugar or an electric urn, creamer, and sugar. They came with or without a tray and they were called the Hostess Set. They carried the catalog numbers 810 for a percolator set or 910 for an urn set. The catalog number designated shapes rather than patterns for these sets. Not to be redundant, I have left pattern numbers off most of this section.

The Platinum sets carried the catalog numbers of 210 for the urn set and 410 for a percolator set. There are two distinct mold differences in these platinum sets. The first being that the top of the percolator spout either comes straight out from the body or at a slightly upward angle. And the second is in the thickness of the percolator handle. It seems to be consistant in that the upward spouted percolators are also the ones with the thicker handles. A good comparison is to look at the White or Pink Flowers versus the Flower Pot or Lavendar Bluebell patterns.

These two shapes began in the early 1930s and were in production through the mid 1940s. A particular pattern may have been discontinued but it was quickly replaced with a different decal on the same shape to make a new pattern.

There are various other shapes of sets and I have included the catalog numbers, where known.

Silhouette Hostess Set

Note that the decals on the sugars and creamers were done in two sizes. I am sure that originally the sets matched but somewhere along the way one or the other was replaced and the decal was the same picture in a different size. It is especially obvious on the percolator set with the Refusal decal. The various decals are covered in the Matched Appliance Sets section under the Colonial pattern. This pattern has not yet been found in the Platinum shape.

Creamer $12.00
Electric percolator 75.00
Electric urn 95.00
Sugar bowl 12.00
Tray, wood (2611) 50.00

Silhouette Hostess urn, sugar, and creamer; Acceptance decal.

Silhouette Hostess percolator, sugar, and creamer; Refusal decal.

Silhouette Hostess urn, sugar, creamer, and wood tray; Bouquet decal.

Black-Eyed Susan Hostess Set

This set was offered in the 1934 Porcelier catalog reprinted in the Reprints section.

Creamer $12.00
Electric percolator 75.00
Electric urn 95.00
Sugar bowl 12.00

Black-eyed Susan
Hostess creamer.

Black-Eyed Susan Percolator Set

This is from the same mid 1930s era as the Hostess sets.

Creamer (710) $12.00
Electric percolator (710) 70.00
Sugar bowl (710) 12.00

Black-eyed Susan percolator.

White and Pink Flower Sets

The White Flower and Pink Flower decals are almost a reversal of the same decal. They have been named for the uppermost flower to ease in identification. One of the confusing things about the sugars and creamers is that they have a white flower on one side and pink on the other. To determine which pattern you have, it is important to face the creamer in the same direction as the electric pot and see if the decal matches. The sugar can be used either way. I have found these sets mismatched many times because of the similarities.

White Flower Hostess Set

This set, consisting of the urn, sugar, and creamer, was featured in the 1938 wholesale catalog of Holsman Company of Chicago, IL, at a cost of $5.40.

Creamer $12.00
Electric percolator 75.00
Electric urn (not shown) 95.00
Sugar bowl 12.00

White Flower Platinum Set

Creamer $8.00
Electric percolator 60.00
Electric urn 95.00
Sugar bowl 8.00

White Flower Platinum urn, percolator, sugar, and creamer.

White Flower Hostess sugar and creamer.

Pink Flower Hostess Set

Creamer $12.00
Electric percolator 75.00
Electric urn (not shown) 95.00
Sugar bowl 12.00

Pink Flower Platinum Set

Creamer $8.00
Electric percolator 60.00
Electric urn (not shown) 95.00
Sugar bowl 8.00

White Flower Hostess percolator, Pink Flower Hostess percolator, sugar, and creamer.

Pink Flower Platinum percolator, sugar, and creamer.

Field Flowers and Reversed Field Flowers Sets

Field Flowers and Reversed Field Flowers are just as confusing as the White Flowers and Pink Flowers. With the use of decals, Porcelier was able to alter patterns by using a portion of a decal or reversing the image to make it look like a new pattern. The only way to be sure everything matches is close inspection for placement of the flowers on each piece. To make matters worse, they had a habit of using the same decals on many different shapes.

There is a water pitcher shown in the Miscellaneous section which has the Field Flower decal.

Field Flowers Hostess Set

Creamer $12.00
Electric percolator 75.00
Electric urn 95.00
Sugar bowl 12.00

Field Flowers Hostess urn, percolator, creamer, and sugar.

Field Flowers Platinum Set

This particular decal and shape was found in a 1938 Holsman Company wholesale catalog. The 3-piece percolator set cost $5.25.

Creamer $8.00
Electric percolator 60.00
Electric urn 95.00
Sugar bowl 8.00

Field Flowers Percolator Set

Creamer (710) $12.00
Electric percolator (710) 75.00
Sugar bowl (710) 12.00

Field Flowers Platinum urn.

Field Flowers Platinum percolator, sugar, and creamer.

Field Flowers percolator, sugar, and creamer (not original glass insert on lid).

Reversed Field Flowers Hostess Set

Creamer $12.00
Electric percolator (not shown) 75.00
Electric urn (not shown) 95.00
Sugar bowl 12.00

Reversed Field Flowers Platinum Set

Creamer $8.00
Electric percolator (not shown) 60.00
Electric urn (not shown) 95.00
Sugar bowl 8.00

Reversed Field Flowers Hostess sugar and creamer.

Reversed Field Flowers Platinum sugar and creamer.

Unnamed Flower Variation

This pattern has not been named and is a variation of Field Flowers. Even though only two pieces have been found, because one is the Hostess shape and the other is the Platinum shape, it is certain that a complete set of each had been made.

Hostess shape:
Creamer (not shown) $12.00
Electric percolator (not shown) 75.00
Electric urn (not shown) 95.00
Sugar bowl 12.00

Platinum shape:
Creamer $8.00
Electric percolator (not shown) 60.00
Electric urn (not shown) 95.00
Sugar bowl (not shown) 8.00

Unnamed Flower Variation Hostess sugar, and Unnamed Flower Variation Platinum creamer.

Orange Poppy Hostess Set

I have not seen a percolator or urn that matches this set. I am positive that they exist because of the make-up of other patterns. They may even exist in the Platinum shape. With the way that Porcelier abbreviated the decals to fit the sugars and creamers, there is no telling what the full decal will look like. I am truly looking forward to this discovery.

Creamer $12.00
Electric percolator (not shown) 75.00
Electric urn (not shown) 95.00
Sugar bowl 12.00

Orange Poppy Hostess sugar and creamer.

There also exists a set which is a cross between the Orange Poppy and the Lavender Bluebell patterns. It has the orange flower from one set with the blue and yellow flowers from the other. This same flower combination is used on the Paneled Orb pattern. Its shape is the same as the Black-eyed Susan percolator set and carries catalog number 710. It has not been named yet.

Flower Pot Sets

The Flower Pot decal has been found on the following three shapes. In addition there is a water pitcher with this decal shown in the Miscellaneous section.

Flower Pot Hostess Set

Creamer $12.00
Electric percolator (not shown) 75.00
Electric urn (not shown) 95.00
Sugar bowl (not shown) 12.00

Flower Pot Hostess creamer.

Flower Pot Platinum Set

Creamer $8.00
Electric percolator 60.00
Electric urn (not shown) 95.00
Sugar bowl 8.00

Flower Pot Platinum Percolator, sugar, and creamer.

Flower Pot Percolator Set

At first glance this percolator seems to be the Platinum shape without the thick platinum lines. Upon closer inspection, the corners are not angled where the platinum would have been, the handle is slightly different, and the front panel is raised slightly from the rest of the body.

Creamer (not shown) $15.00
Electric percolator 70.00
Sugar bowl (not shown) 15.00

Flower Pot percolator.

Lavender Bluebell Platinum Set

This set has not yet been found in the Hostess shape. It is from the early 1930s and was found in a National-Porges wholesale catalog dated 1933. The percolator was $4.07. If you wanted the sugar and creamer too, it was $5.14 for the 3-piece set. Note the variations of the sugar and creamer decals on the two sets shown.

Creamer $8.00
Electric percolator 60.00
Electric urn 95.00
Sugar bowl 8.00

Lavender Bluebell Platinum percolator, sugar, and creamer.

Lavender Bluebell Platinum urn, sugar, and creamer.

Antique Rose Platinum Set

This set looks like the standard Platinum set. However, I want to point out that its lid, which is original, does not have the standard glass insert found on most of the Hostess and Platinum sets.

Creamer $8.00
Electric percolator 60.00
Electric urn (not shown) 95.00
Sugar bowl 8.00

Antique Rose Deco Set

This set has a much more art deco look to it than any of the other percolator sets. It combines features from the Platinum and Serv-All sets to the Antique Rose decal making for a very unique pattern.

Creamer (not shown) $10.00
Electric percolator 65.00
Sugar bowl (not shown) 10.00

Antique Rose Platinum percolator, sugar, and creamer.

Antique Rose Deco percolator.

Cattail Hostess Set

This set is very similar to the Cattail set made by the Hall China Company for Westinghouse. On occasion, I have seen this mismarked as Hall China in antiques shops. It is not known whether it was made in the Platinum shape or not.

Creamer $15.00
Electric percolator (not shown) 80.00
Electric urn (not shown) 100.00
Sugar bowl 15.00

Cattail Hostess sugar and creamer.

Golden Fuchsia Platinum Set

The Golden Fuchsia has only been found in the Platinum shape thus far. It has however, been found in either black or aqua. The insides of these pieces are the same color as the exterior.

Creamer $20.00
Electric percolator 85.00
Sugar bowl 20.00

Golden Fuchsia sugar, percolator, and creamer in black. Photo courtesy of Gary and Myrna Stewart.

Golden Fuchsia sugar and creamer in aqua. Photo courtesy of Frank Simonie.

Miniature Rose Percolator Set

In my opinion, this is one of the most elegant sets they made. The artistry and beauty of the design attests to the quality of Porcelier. This pattern makes heavy use of gold detailing to add to the elegance. It is from the late 1940s.

Creamer $15.00
Electric percolator (50) 95.00
Sugar bowl 15.00

Miniature Rose percolator, sugar, and creamer.

Floral Panel Percolator Set

This set once again makes use of the White Flower and Pink Flower decals. Because of the hand decorating, the manner in which the gold has been applied on the design may vary. Some of the lids have three gold lines around them while others have only one.

Creamer $12.00
Electric percolator (70) 75.00
Sugar bowl 12.00

Floral Panel percolator, sugar, and creamer.

Tulips Percolator Set

This is another elegant set which was made in the late 1940s. The finials and the bottom border, which is an embossed leaf pattern, comes tinted in a pale pink or pale blue. The finials are shaped like tulips and it has gold detailing.

Creamer $18.00
Electric percolator (10) 85.00
Sugar bowl 18.00

Tulips percolator, sugar, and creamer in pale pink.

Tulips sugar and creamer in pale blue.

53

Bell Flower Percolator Set

The Bell Flower is named for its painted flowers at the top border. The embossed loops on the bodies of the sugar and creamer follow through on the percolator as well. This too, was detailed in gold as was the general practice on Porcelier's more elegant sets.

Creamer $15.00
Electric percolator 80.00
Sugar bowl 15.00

Bell Flower sugar and creamer.

Fleur-de-Lis Percolator Set

The Fleur-de-lis has a much different look. The shape, colors, and lid design tend to suggest an early to mid 1930s period. The spouts are accented with a raised leaf pattern.

Creamer $15.00
Electric percolator (2607) 80.00
Sugar bowl 15.00

Fleur-de-lis percolator, sugar, and creamer.

Leaf and Shadow

This electric set was made in the early 1950s. It is one of the last electric sets made by Porcelier and there seems to be an abundance of them in the Western Pennsylvania area. The percolator with the short handle was not as plentiful.

Note the differences in the spouts, handles, and body color of these two percolators. I have not found a sugar and creamer to match the short-handled design but suspect that they are out there.

The rhomboidal-shaped teapot has been used for three different patterns: the Leaf and Shadow, Dainty Rose, and Solid Maroon. The latter two are shown in the Single Pots section.

The lid shape has been duplicated on the aforementioned pots and again on the Dogwood II pattern.

Creamer $12.00
Electric percolator, long handle (31) 75.00
Electric percolator, short handle 85.00
Sugar bowl 12.00
4-cup pot (green, gray, or black trim) 28.00

Leaf and Shadow percolator (short handle), percolator (long handle), sugar, and creamer.

Leaf and Shadow 4-cup teapots, green and gray.

Starflower Percolator

Looking very similar in shape to the short-handled Leaf and Shadow set, the Starflower has an altogether different handle. Its body is more creamy than white in color. The decoration is hand painted and it dates from the early 1950s.

A sugar and creamer in this pattern have not yet been verified.

Electric percolator (120) $70.00

Starflower percolator.

Golden Wheat Percolator

This is another variation of hand painting on the same shape as the Starflower percolator. It is also from the early 1950s.

The matching sugar and creamer have not been verified.

Electric percolator (120) $70.00

Golden Wheat percolator.

Solid Percolator

This Solid percolator is very close in shape to the Solid tankard-shaped pot shown in the Single Pots and Pitchers section. It is the only piece that has been found to date and it has a clip on lid as detailed in the Reprints section under patents.

Electric percolator $65.00

Solid percolator.

Flight

This is also called "Ducks" or "Geese" by some collectors. It was designed by Carl Kobler, an in-house designer.

The embossed pattern depicts birds in flight above cattails. The air-brushed clouds vary in the shade of blue due to the hand decorating. The lid is the same as on the Mexican, Beehive Floral Spray, and Flamingo sets. Flight was introduced in the late 1930s and was still being sold by Sears, Roebuck & Company in the late 1940s and early 1950s. In 1938 a 6-cup pot retailed for $.98 while the pot with sugar and creamer was $1.49.

This pattern is plentiful due to the length of time it was made. It is especially popular today, because of its wildlife theme.

In the Novelty section of this book there are more pieces of this pattern which were not made for resale.

Creamer $16.00
Disc pitcher 85.00
Electric percolator (2407) 85.00
Sugar bowl 16.00
2-cup pot 45.00
4-cup pot 40.00
6-cup pot 40.00
8-cup pot 50.00

Flight percolator, sugar, and creamer.

Flight 2-cup pot, 4-cup pot with dripper, 6-cup pot, and 8-cup pot.

Flight disc pitcher.

Double Floral

Characterized by a raised bar down the center of the pot with two or three flowers on either side, this is the only pattern I have found where there was a definite teapot made, besides the four sizes which could be used as either a coffee pot or teapot. The teapot is a 4-cup size and the close-up picture shows the lid opening for the teapot on the left versus the coffee pot on the right.

At the last minute, a creamer in this shape, with two decaled pink roses has surfaced. It has a platinum stripe around the top and bottom edges. Unfortunately, there was not enough time to include a picture of it in the book.

Creamer $12.00
Electric percolator (7007) 75.00
Sugar bowl 12.00
2-cup pot 35.00
4-cup pot (coffee or tea) 30.00
6-cup pot 30.00
8-cup pot 35.00

Double Floral percolator, sugar, and creamer.

Double Floral 2-cup pot, 4-cup pot with dripper, 6-cup pot, and 8-cup pot with dripper.

Left: 4-cup teapot lid opening.
Right: 4-cup coffee pot lid opening.

Smaller Kitchen Sets

These sets contain more than the standard four sizes of pots and sugar bowl/creamer sets, but do not have any electrical pieces in them. They do, however, have some accessory pieces.

1939 New York World's Fair

Made for the 1939 New York World's Fair this pattern has become harder to find because of the collectibility of World's Fair items. When they are found, the prices have been pushed way beyond that of a normal piece. They have not yet skyrocketed out of reach, as the Hall China New York World's Fair teapot has.

There have been rumors of a drink coaster, a third size of disc pitcher, and an electric percolator in this pattern but none of these have been confirmed. I was told by many past employees that the company gave every employee a New York World's Fair pitcher as a gift when these were made.

Ashtray	$100.00 – 150.00
Creamer	.80.00 – 100.00
Sugar bowl	.80.00 – 100.00
5" disc pitcher	125.00 – 150.00
7" disc pitcher	175.00 – 250.00
2-cup pot (not shown)	225.00 – 300.00
4-cup pot	225.00 – 300.00
6-cup pot	200.00 – 250.00
8-cup pot	200.00 – 250.00

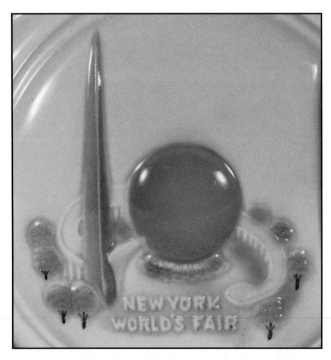

Close-up of the design taken from the disc pitcher.

1939 New York World's Fair ashtray (unmarked).

1939 New York World's Fair 4-cup pot without lid, 6-cup pot, and 8-cup pot.

1939 New York World's Fair sugar and creamer.

1939 New York World's Fair 5" disc pitcher and 7" disc pitcher.

Mexican

Also known as Sante Fe by collectors. This is one of the most confusing patterns to collect because of the difficulty in determining the sizes. I have personally purchased four of the 6-cup size, thinking each time that I was getting an 8-cup pot.

Differences to note are that the 2-cup does not have the rickrack trim around the top or bottom and has the Mexican and the cactus. The 4-cup has the trim, the Mexican, and the cactus. The 6- and 8-cup have the trim, the Mexican on a burro, and cacti.

I have pictured one of the fancier pots with the sugar and creamer to show how much more detail some of these pots were painted with. They include the rickrack done in an orange and green combination rather than all orange, trim on the Mexican's sombrero and clothes, a fancier serape, eyes and hooves on the burro, and grass under their feet.

This has the same lid as the Flight, Beehive Floral Spray, and the Flamingo sets. It was designed by Carl Kobler, an in-house designer.

I was told by a collector that he had seen an electric percolator for this set some time ago but this has not been confirmed. The drip pots were sold by Sears, Roebuck & Company in the 1940s. In 1942 the 6-cup pot sold for $.98, the sugar and creamer for $.69, and the 3-piece set for $1.49.

Ball jug $80.00
Creamer 15.00
Sugar bowl 15.00
2-cup pot 45.00
4-cup pot 40.00
6-cup pot 40.00
8-cup pot 50.00

Mexican ball jug.

Mexican (fancy) 6-cup pot, sugar, and creamer.

Mexican 2-cup pot, 4-cup pot, 6-cup pot, and 8-cup pot.

Oriental Deco

We began by calling this Hot Art Deco because it almost looked as if the word "hot" was hidden in the printing down the side of the pot. It was later decided that it really has more of an Oriental style and that name seemed to fit better.

Note that the loop design of the handles is carried through to the shakers.

Creamer $12.00	6-cup boiler 45.00
Decanter 60.00	8-cup boiler 45.00
	2-cup pot 40.00
Shakers	4-cup pot 35.00
flour, pepper, salt and sugar (each) . .15.00	6-cup pot 35.00
Sugar bowl 12.00	8-cup pot 40.00
4-cup boiler (not shown) 40.00	

Oriental Deco 2-cup pot, 4-cup pot, 6-cup pot, and 8-cup pot.

Oriental Deco sugar and creamer.

Oriental Deco 6-cup boiler in pan and 8-cup boiler without pan.

Oriental Deco decanter.

Oriental Deco shaker set.

Country Life Series

Based on just knowing about the 2-cup pot for the longest time, I was calling this Cottage. Another collector found the 6- and 8-cup pots and was calling it Girl at the Well. Once it was put together that these were the same pattern, neither name fit. Thus the change to Country Life Series.

The four distinct pictures on this set are all tied together with the color scheme, the embossed borders, the finials, and the fluting on the lids. The sugar, creamer, and casserole show a cobblestone path, fence, and a cottage roof in the distance. The 2- and 4-cup pots show a cottage at the end of a cobblestone path. The 6- and 8-cup pots have a girl at a well.

The canister has no picture on it, but it does have the heart border and a fluted lid. The knob on the canisters may match either the casserole or the teapot lids and still be correct. I have seen the three canisters listed below but there may be others, such as salt and coffee.

I am listing only a large size of the casserole since that has been verified. However, other patterns are known to have two sizes in the casserole so it is possible that a smaller one exists.

Canisters:
    flour, sugar, and utility (each) $35.00
Casserole, w/lid, 9½" 85.00
Creamer 15.00
Sugar bowl 15.00
2-cup pot 40.00
4-cup pot (not shown) 35.00
6-cup pot 45.00
8-cup pot 50.00

Country Life Series flour canister, lid knob matches casserole.

Country Life Series sugar canister, lid knob matches pots.

Country Life Series sugar, creamer, and 2-cup pot without lid.

Country Life Series 6-cup pot and 8-cup pot.

Country Life Series 9½" covered casserole.

Hearth

The Hearth, designed by Carl Kobler, is also referred to as the "Fireplace." It is embossed with a fireplace, chair, oval rug, cat, and spinning wheel. There are vertical lines coming up about 1" on the flared bottom all the way around the pot creating a fluted look. The lid has a flat round finial and it may be fluted or plain. This pot comes in two distinct body colors, white or cream. It has also been made with gold or platinum trim. This pattern is a very common one as it was sold by Sears, Roebuck & Company during the mid to late 1940s.

The sugar and creamer depict a dressing table with a lamp and a picture on the wall. It is trimmed around the bottom and lid in the same manner as the pots.

I have seen a picture of this pot painted completely red but have not personally inspected it to confirm its authenticity.

Copies have been made of the pots and sugar bowl. There is also a canister set done in the same pattern by unknown makers. See Reproductions and Takeoffs for more details.

Creamer $10.00
Disc pitcher 70.00
Sugar bowl 10.00
2-cup pot 30.00
4-cup pot 30.00
6-cup pot 30.00
8-cup pot 30.00

*Add $10.00 per piece for gold or platinum trim.

Row 1: Hearth sugar, creamer, 2-cup pot, and 6-cup pot with dripper.
Row 2: 4-cup pot with dripper, disc pitcher, and 8-cup pot.

Basketweave Cameo

This is one of the many variations of a basketweave that was so popular with Porcelier. Because of the number of pieces in this set, it is a most collectible pattern. There are light fixtures to match shown in the Lighting Fixture section.

Bean pot, individual $10.00
Canisters:
  flour, sugar, and utility (each) 35.00
Casserole, w/lid, 6¾" (not shown) 45.00
Casserole, w/lid, 8½" 55.00
Creamer 12.00
Sugar bowl 12.00
2-cup pot (not shown) 35.00
4-cup pot 30.00
6-cup pot 35.00
8-cup pot (not shown) 45.00

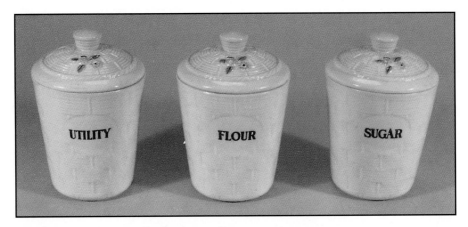

Basketweave Cameo canister set.

Basketweave Cameo sugar and creamer.

Basketweave Cameo 4-cup pot and 6-cup pot.

Basketweave Cameo 8½" covered casserole and individual bean pot.

Rope Bow

The Rope Bow has also been called "Bow Knot" and "Drape." It is characterized by a rope around the top and bottom of the pot being tied into bows on the front giving a gathered look to the body of the pot. The finial also has a rope effect around it.

The only accessory pieces found to date have been the two sizes of the double boilers. I have heard rumors of a small pitcher but it has not been confirmed.

<pre>
Creamer $12.00
Sugar bowl 12.00
6-cup boiler 35.00
8-cup boiler 40.00
2-cup pot (not shown) 40.00
4-cup pot 35.00
6-cup pot 35.00
8-cup pot 40.00
</pre>

Rope Bow sugar and creamer.

Rope Bow 6- and 8-cup boilers.

Rope Bow 4-cup pot, 6-cup pot, and 8-cup pot.

Beehive Crisscross

Named for its shape, it resembles a beehive with embossed diamond patterns and a flower in the center diamond. The flowers on the sugar and creamer are slightly different than on the other pieces. The finial is similar to a monkey's fist knot.

Ball jug $70.00
Creamer 12.00
Sugar bowl .12.00
2-cup pot (not shown) 40.00
4-cup pot 35.00
6-cup pot 35.00
8-cup pot (not shown) 40.00

Row 1: Beehive Crisscross sugar, 4-cup pot, and creamer.
Row 2: Ball jug and 6-cup pot.

Beehive Floral Spray

This is another beehive shape without the diamonds. There are two sprigs of flowers extending down from the top of the pieces. The lid is the same as on the Flight, Mexican, and Flamingo sets.

Ball jug $70.00
Creamer 10.00
Sugar bowl .10.00
4-cup boiler .35.00
2-cup pot 40.00
4-cup pot 35.00
6-cup pot 35.00
8-cup pot (not shown) 40.00

Beehive Floral Spray 2-cup pot with dripper, 4-cup pot, and 6-cup pot.

Beehive Floral Spray, 4-cup boiler and ball jug.

Beehive Floral Spray sugar and creamer.

Non-Electric Coffee and Teapot Sets

These are strictly coffee and teapot sets. There are no confirmed accessory pieces to these patterns. They may have one to four sizes of pots and a sugar and creamer set in their composition.

Nautical

Perhaps one of the most well-known and common patterns Porcelier produced, Nautical was sold through mail-order catalogs such as Montgomery Wards. It appears in their catalogs from the early 1940s until 1950. The 6-cup pot was priced at $1.79 from 1942 until 1950 (the last year offered) when it went to $1.98.

Also designed by Carl Kobler and called "Sailboat" or "Ships" by collectors, it carries out the nautical theme with embossed ships in full sail on blue water. There is a border of anchors and life buoys running around the top rim of the pot. The finial may be a life buoy shape or a standard flat round shape. Either one could be an original lid as it is shown both ways in catalog reprints. The finish can be white or cream and there are many variations with gold or platinum trim.

Be aware that copies of this pattern have been made by an unknown maker. See the section on Reproductions and Takeoffs for more details.

Creamer	$20.00
Sugar bowl	20.00
2-cup pot	40.00
4-cup pot	30.00
6-cup pot	30.00
8-cup pot	35.00

*Add $10.00 per piece for gold or platinum trim.

Nautical gold-trimmed sugar, 2-cup pot with decorated dripper, and creamer.

Nautical 2-cup pot with dripper, 4-cup pot with dripper, 6-cup pot, and 8-cup pot.

Nautical sugar and creamer.

Nautical gold-trimmed 6-cup pot.

Nautical gold-trimmed sugar and creamer.

Dutch Boy and Girl

This pattern is embossed with a Dutch boy and girl holding hands in the center, each holding a flower in their other hand. There are two flowers below them and one above. There is an embossed border of leaves and vine running all the way around the top and bottom. The body is ivory or white. The lid may have an arched knob or the standard flat round finial. There have been gold and platinum decorated pieces made in this pattern.

The pattern of the sugar bowl and creamer is the same leaf and vine border on top and bottom with three flowers on the front which match those on the pots.

There is a matching lamp shown in the Lighting Fixtures section of the book. These were a creation of Carl Kobler, an in-house designer of Porcelier.

This has also been referred to as "Dolls," "Dutch Couple," or "Dutch Wedding." Montgomery Wards carried this pattern from the early 1940s until 1950. Its pricing was identical to the Nautical pattern. It is considered to be another of the common patterns as it is easily found.

Creamer $8.00
Sugar bowl 8.00
2-cup pot — boy (not shown) 45.00
2-cup pot — girl 30.00
4-cup pot 30.00
6-cup pot 30.00
8-cup pot 30.00

*Add $10.00 per piece for gold or platinum trim.

Row 1: Dutch Boy and Girl sugar, creamer, and 2-cup pot with dripper.
Row 2: 4-cup pot with dripper, 6-cup pot, and 8-cup pot.

Dutch Boy and Girl 6-cup pot with gold trim.

Flamingo

There are two distinct molds of this pattern. A close-up of the detail difference is shown below. Note that the pot on the left with the darker flamingo is not as graceful and the water and plants are not very well defined. The right one has much more detail in the body of the flamingo itself and a crisscross pattern in the water. This seems to hold true based on the flamingo coloring. The reason for the two molds is unknown.

The lid is the same as appears on the Flight, Mexican, and the Beehive Floral Spray sets. It is from the late 1930s – early 1940s and has been seen in both the wholesale Holsman Company and the retail Spiegel catalogs. In 1938 a 3-piece set wholesaled for $.88.

```
Creamer . . . . . . . . . . . . . . . . . . . . . . .$10.00
Sugar bowl  . . . . . . . . . . . . . . . . . . . . .10.00
2-cup pot . . . . . . . . . . . . . . . . . . . . . .40.00
4-cup pot . . . . . . . . . . . . . . . . . . . . . .40.00
6-cup pot . . . . . . . . . . . . . . . . . . . . . .40.00
8-cup pot . . . . . . . . . . . . . . . . . . . . . .40.00
```

Row 1: Flamingo sugar, creamer, 2-cup pot with dripper. Row 2: 4-cup pot, 6-cup pot, and 8-cup pot.

Close-up of Flamingo mold variation detail.

76

Pears

This shape is embossed with pears, cherries, leaves, and a star; has no border decoration; and the handle goes from top to bottom. This shape was also used for the Dancing Boy & Girl, Magnolia, and Southern Belle sets. It is short and squat compared to most of the other patterns made by Porcelier.

Pears came in a 2-color or 5-color decoration. I have not seen a sugar or creamer in the 2-color style. I do not feel that the coloring affects the pricing on this pattern.

Creamer $15.00
Sugar bowl 15.00
2-cup pot 30.00
4-cup pot 25.00
6-cup pot 25.00
8-cup pot 30.00

Row 1: Pears sugar, creamer, and 2-cup pot with dripper.
Row 2: 4-cup pot, 6-cup pot with dripper, and 8-cup pot.
All are 5-color designs except the 4-cup pot shown.

Close-up of Pears for comparison between 5-color (on left) and 2-color (on right) designs.

Cobblestone I and II

Designed by Chauncey E. Waltman of Chicago, IL, in 1935, and assigned to Porcelier. Embossed to represent a stone wall, it has a girl standing in front of the wall. There are several flowers growing beside her and she is holding more. The pattern of stones is continued in the handle, spout, and cover of this pot. This same theme is copied in Cobblestone II with variations in the girl's hat, apron, and the flowers. I believe the sugar and creamer were made to match either style. The prices are the same for either pattern.

Creamer $15.00
Sugar bowl 15.00
2-cup pot 35.00
4-cup pot 30.00
6-cup pot 30.00
8-cup pot 35.00

Row 1: Cobblestone sugar, creamer, and Cobblestone I 2-cup pot. Row 2: Cobblestone I 4-cup pot, 6-cup pot, and 8-cup pot.

Cobblestone II 6- and 8-cup pots.

Basketweave Floral

This particular basketweave design comes with either a brown or colored floral pattern at the top of the pieces. Because of the hand painting, no two designs are identical. As mentioned earlier, this is another of the few patterns that has a matching decorated dripper.

Creamer $10.00
Sugar bowl 10.00
2-cup pot (not shown) 35.00
4-cup pot (not shown) 35.00
6-cup pot 30.00
6-cup pot w/decorated dripper 55.00
8-cup pot 30.00

Basketweave Floral 6-cup brown pot, 6-cup colored pot, and 8-cup colored pot.

Basketweave Floral colored sugar and creamer.

Basketweave Floral colored 6-cup pot with decorated dripper.

Medallion

The Medallion has a basket of flowers inside a medallion painted on the center of the pot. There is a ring of green leaves around the medallion and a tied-back drapery on either side. Just above it is an embossed, uncolored Fleur-de-lis. The border around the rim resembles a rope and there is a brown line around the pot and lid.

Creamer $10.00
Sugar bowl 10.00
6-cup pot 30.00

Medallion 6-cup pot.

Medallion sugar and creamer.

Ribbed Cameo Flower Basket

Another flower basket adorns the cameo in the center of this pattern. The basket is painted on while the cameo and ribs are embossed. The finial looks somewhat like a pretzel.

Creamer $10.00
Sugar bowl 10.00
6-cup pot 30.00

Ribbed Cameo Flower Basket sugar, 6-cup pot, and creamer.

Rose and Wheat

Named for the center pink rose and stalk of wheat, this set is highly embossed. It carries the standard flat round lid.

In the following picture, the sugar bowl is missing its lid but it originally came with one.

Creamer $10.00
Sugar bowl 10.00
2-cup pot 30.00
4-cup pot 25.00
6-cup pot 25.00
8-cup pot (not shown) 30.00

Row 1: Rose and Wheat sugar (missing lid), creamer, and 2-cup pot.
Row 2: 4-cup pot with dripper and 6-cup pot.

Paneled Rose

This also is being called Pear Blossom due to the unusual finial. This pattern depicts a rose among other flowers placed in the center front panel. The panels go all the way around the pot. The lid and spout have a molded border of pears and leaves while the finial is an orange pear.

There are light fixtures with the same center floral design shown in the Lighting Fixtures section.

Creamer $12.00
Sugar bowl .12.00
2-cup pot (not shown) 35.00
4-cup pot 30.00
6-cup pot 30.00
8-cup pot 35.00

Paneled Rose 4-cup pot, 6-cup pot, and 8-cup pot.

Paneled Rose sugar and creamer.

Floral Trio

The flowers on this French Drip set are embossed. Its rim is scalloped and the finial is a plain ball. The sugar bowl lid is identical to the lid of the pots.

This has been seen in both the 1938 Montgomery Wards and Holsman Company catalogs. Holsman sold a 6-cup pot for $.88 and a 3-piece set for $1.47 in 1938.

Creamer $15.00
Sugar bowl 15.00
2-cup pot 35.00
4-cup pot (not shown) 30.00
6-cup pot 30.00
8-cup pot (not shown) 35.00

Floral Trio 2-cup pot and 6-cup pot.

Floral Trio sugar (missing lid) and creamer.

Paneled Orb

The name may be a little strange but this was one of the latest discoveries and it came near the completion of the book. It is characterized by an orb shape and vertical lines beginning about one third of the way from the top and running to the bottom creating a paneled effect. There is a decal of multicolored flowers on the top one third of the pot. It has a plain round finial.

Creamer $12.00
Sugar bowl 12.00
6-cup pot 30.00

Paneled Orb sugar, 6-cup pot, and creamer.

Goldfinches

Also known as Canaries and Yellow Bird, this pattern features two yellow birds with black wings sitting on a branch with blue flowers. Once again the standard flat round finial is used. The sugar and creamer have solid handles in the same shape as the pots but only show the branch of flowers.

I was told by a decorator that the first of these made had only one leg painted on the front goldfinch. The decorators thought it looked odd and brought it to the attention of a foreman. It was changed and two legs were painted on subsequent pots. Interestingly enough, after checking over my own pots, I discovered that there indeed was a difference in this exact detail. After that out-of-the-blue revelation how could her story be doubted?

Creamer $12.00
Sugar bowl 12.00
2-cup pot (not shown) 30.00
4-cup pot 25.00
6-cup pot 25.00
8-cup pot 30.00

Goldfinches 4-cup pot, 6-cup pot with dripper, and 8-cup pot.

Goldfinches sugar and creamer.

Tree Trunk

This unique pot was designed by Chauncey E. Waltman of Chicago, IL, and assigned to Porcelier in 1935. Collectors have also referred to this pot as Tree Stump. The pattern is a molded relief of a tree trunk complete with bark and knotholes. The finial is similar to a sawed-off branch of a tree.

Creamer $15.00
Sugar bowl 15.00
2-cup pot 40.00
4-cup pot (not shown) 35.00
6-cup pot 35.00
8-cup pot 40.00

Tree Trunk 2-cup pot, 6-cup pot, and 8-cup pot.

Tree Trunk sugar and creamer.

Log Cabin

This is another design by Chauncey E. Waltman of Chicago, IL. It was assigned to Porcelier in 1935. It depicts a log cabin with a chimney for a finial. The creamer and sugar bowl are smaller versions of the main pot rather than an abbreviated form.

Creamer $15.00
Sugar bowl 15.00
2-cup pot (not shown) 40.00
4-cup pot 35.00
6-cup pot 35.00
8-cup pot (not shown) 40.00

Row 1: Log Cabin sugar and creamer.
Row 2: 4-cup pot and 6-cup pot.

Tomato

This is one of the most different and unexpected patterns by Porcelier. Its total red color just does not fit the Porcelier image. Another big difference is that it was cold-painted so it scratches quite easily. I have been told that if you apply a light coat of clear glaze (often found in craft stores) it will not scratch so quickly.

Creamer $15.00
Sugar bowl 15.00
2-cup pot (not shown) 35.00
4-cup pot 30.00
6-cup pot 30.00
8-cup pot (not shown) 35.00

Tomato sugar, creamer,
4- and 6-cup pots.

Chevron

This is a most frustrating pattern. It must have been a very popular shape as they certainly like to make variations of it. It is a basic teapot shape but has raised panels on the corners which are embossed with a pattern resembling a chevron. The center was then decorated with a brown transfer print, a colored transfer print, the White Flower decal, or a stylized orange flower. Some of the chevron panels were highlighted with various shades of orange. Other decorations may surface yet.

There has not been confirmation of a 4-cup pot or a sugar and creamer to match.

2-cup pitcher	$25.00
2-cup pot	35.00
3-cup pot	25.00
6-cup pot	35.00
8-cup pot	35.00

Chevron 6-cup pot, brown design; and 8-cup pot, colored design.

Chevron 8-cup pot with White Flower decal.

Chevron 2-cup pot with Stylized Orange flower.

87

Chevron 2-cup pitcher with brown design.

Orange Chevron 3-cup teapot.

American Beauty Rose

I have heard comments about this looking like a Hall China piece. It truly is Porcelier and carries their bottom stamp to prove it. The simple shape, rose decal, and gold trim combine perfectly to make this a striking set. This also has been found undecorated in the ivory color.

Creamer $12.00
Sugar bowl 12.00
6-cup pot 35.00

American Beauty Rose sugar, 6-cup pot, and creamer.

Geometric Cattails

These have 8 or 10 facets to the body and can tier to the top with one or two sections. The handles can be square or have a notch at the corner. The lids are sectioned from the finial outward in 8 or 10 sections and the finial is a flattened ball. The cattails are hand painted on each section. Because of this, they may vary slightly from one panel to the next or from one pot to the next.

Creamer (not shown) $12.00
Sugar bowl (not shown) 12.00
2-cup pitcher 25.00
2-cup pot (not shown) 35.00
4-cup pot (not shown) 35.00
6-cup pot 30.00
8-cup pot 30.00

Geometric Cattails 2-cup pitcher (square handle), 6-cup pot with dripper (square handle), and 8-cup pot (notched handle).

Geometric Wheat

Similar to the Geometric Cattails in style these have a sprig of wheat rather than a cattail decoration. Another difference is that the finial is a small arch instead of a flattened ball. These have only been found with the notched handle but it stands to reason that they probably exist with a square handle too.

Creamer $12.00
Sugar bowl 12.00
2-cup pot 35.00
4-cup pot 35.00
6-cup pot 30.00
8-cup pot (not shown) 30.00

Geometric Wheat 2-cup pot, 4-cup pot, and 6-cup pot (notched handles).

Geometric Wheat sugar and creamer (notched handle).

89

Color Band

The Color Band looks more like a restaurant type of ware. It has been found with either a yellow or dark green band and has a sugar and creamer to match. I have heard a rumor of a fuchsia color but it has not been confirmed.

Creamer $8.00
Sugar bowl (not shown) 8.00
2-cup pot 25.00
4-cup pot 25.00
6-cup pot (not shown) 25.00
8-cup pot (not shown) 25.00

Color Band 2-cup green pot with dripper and 4-cup yellow pot.

Color Band green creamer.

Harlequin

Harlequin has a shape of its own even though the lid is similar to Pears, Southern Belle, Magnolia, and Dancing Boy and Girl. It has two distinct patterns, large or small triangles, and has been found in color combinations of black/blue, black/burgundy, and black/dark green. I have not confirmed sugar and creamer sets to match, but have heard of their existence.

4-cup small design $30.00
6-cup small design (not shown) 35.00
6-cup large design 35.00

Harlequin 4-cup pot (small black/blue design) and 6-cup pot (large black/blue design).

Harlequin 6-cup pot (large black/burgundy design).

Harlequin 6-cup pot (large black/dark green design).

Single Pots and Pitchers

For the most part, the items included in this category are things for which only one size of a given pattern has been found. They may require reclassification if more pieces, such as a sugar and creamer, surface and dictate that they were part of a set. As with everything made by Porcelier, just when you thought you had it figured out, something new would arise and throw your theory all to pieces.

Southern Belle

This is the same shape as the Pears, Dancing Boy and Girl, and the Magnolia patterns. So far it has been found in three color variations. I have only seen the woman's dress in yellow, but the gentleman's tuxedo has variations as do the flowers and window frame. It would not be surprising if this showed up with a pink dress.

6-cup pot $40.00

Southern Belle 6-cup pots in three color variations.

Magnolia

The only variation discovered on the Magnolia so far is the center of the flower being yellow or orange. It shares the shape of the Pears, Southern Belle, and Dancing Boy and Girl patterns.

6-cup pot $35.00

Magnolia 6-cup pot with yellow center.

Dancing Boy and Girl

This particular pot is from a past employee of Porcelier and he assured me that this was painted especially for him. The ones made for resale were done in pastel colors, as was usual for Porcelier. Unfortunately, he could not remember what colors those were. It will be exciting to locate one to discover what it looks like.

6-cup pot, pastel $40.00

Dancing Boy and Girl 6-cup pot in gold decoration.

Dainty Rose

One of the three rhomboidal-shaped pots made, this sports the unusual background color of apple green. It has a lid as on Leaf and Shadow, Daisy Teardrop, and Dogwood II.

4-cup pot $40.00

Dainty Rose 4-cup pot.

Solid Maroon

This was obtained from a long-time Porcelier employee and she was not sure if this was a test piece or if it was actually made for resale in this color. Even though the shape is shared with other patterns, the lid is unique. It is square with a square finial. Note that the edge lines of the color are not as clean as one would expect on an item for resale.

4-cup pot $25.00

Solid Maroon 4-cup pot.

Periwinkle

This very definitely has the look of a teapot. It has been found with a dark green or black background. The flowers have been a constant periwinkle blue. The lid is repeated on the Latticework, Flute & Curl, and Dogwood I teapots.

4-cup pot $30.00

Periwinkle 4-cup pots in dark green and black.

Latticework

Another delicate teapot, the Latticework is embellished with a raised flower at each cross in the pattern. It has been found in yellow or pale green. The lid is interchangeable with the lids of the Periwinkle, Flute & Curl, and the Dogwood I pots.

4-cup pot $30.00

Latticework 4-cup pots in pale green and yellow.

Flute & Curl

Known to exist in yellow or pale green, this pattern has the same lid as the Periwinkle, Latticework, and Dogwood I patterns.

4-cup pot $35.00

Flute & Curl 4-cup pot in pale green.

Daisy Teardrop

This unusual shape has an upper rim similar to a Peter Pan collar of a woman's blouse. The same lid appears on the Leaf and Shadow, Dainty Rose, and Dogwood II teapots. There are raised daisies inside the teardrop shape on the front of the pot. The teardrop is dark green with gold trim.

4-cup pot $40.00

Daisy Teardrop 4-cup pot.

Dogwood I

Called Red or Purple Dogwood by collectors, it has now shown up with a yellow dogwood. It has been found with both yellow and pale green trim and carries the same lid as Periwinkle, Latticework, and Flute & Curl designs. Some have been trimmed in gold.

4-cup pot $30.00

Dogwood I 4-cup pots red flower/yellow trim, red flower/yellow and gold trim, and red flower/pale green trim.

Dogwood I 4-cup pot yellow flower/yellow and gold trim (Dogwood II type finial).

Dogwood II

Another teapot shape carrying the same lid as Leaf and Shadow, Dainty Rose, and Daisy Teardrop, this has been found with yellow or dark green trim or completely black. The painted flowers could be yellow, pink, or a yellow/fuchsia combination.

4-cup pot $30.00
4-cup pot, black .55.00

Dogwood II 4-cup pots yellow flower/yellow trim, yellow and fuchsia flower/black pot, and pink flower/green trim.

Deco Ribbed

This pot has a much more yellow tint to the main body. It is highlighted with orange bands around the bottom, handle, spout centers, the finial, and along the upper rim of the pot. The ribs run vertically around the pot and radiate out from the center of the lid. It has a very art deco look.

6-cup pot $35.00

Deco Ribbed 6-cup pot.

Rooster

This strange pot has been a frustration to collectors. I know that many do not have a correct lid and have been hunting furiously to find one.

The scene is the classical rooster on a fence, crowing in the sunrise. The finial has a touch of green to match the green of the fields.

I also have been speculating as to whether or not this had a matching sugar and creamer. If they do exist, I do not know what to expect them to look like.

6-cup pot $55.00

Rooster 6-cup pot.

Cameo Floral

This teapot is the only pattern, known to date, that is oval in shape. It has delicate raised flowers and swirls around the center cameo. There are floral cameos on the lid and more raised swirls. The pattern is repeated on both sides.

6-cup pot $45.00

Cameo Floral 6-cup pot.

Blue Roses

This has a ribbed border around the top and bottom of the pot with a band of alternating blue roses and brown leaves around the center. The finial is a small arch shape.

6-cup pot $40.00

Blue Roses 6-cup pot.

Orange Trellis

These two pots seem to have been done on a similar theme along with the Orange Chevron and Brown Medallion pots. They each have their own shape but are characterized by an orange or butterscotch shading which has been airbrushed on to highlight the raised designs.

Round:
3-cup pot $25.00

Sculptured:
3-cup pot $25.00

Orange Chevron

3-cup pot $25.00

Brown Medallion

3-cup pot $30.00

Brown medallion, Orange Trellis Sculptured, Orange Trellis Round, and Orange Chevron. (All are 3-cup pots.)

99

Trellis

The Trellis pattern seemed to be very popular and easy to alter to create a new pattern. The following pots have either a top or bottom trellis design and usually incorporate some sort of transfer print in conjunction with the trellis. There may be other variations than those shown.

Trellis Top:
6-cup pot $30.00

Trellis Bottom:
6-cup pot $30.00

Cameo Trellis:
6-cup pot $30.00

Trellis Top 6-cup pot.

Trellis Bottom 6-cup pot.

Cameo Trellis 6-cup pots with variations.

Ribbed Bottom

This shape is a French Drip coffee maker, Catalog No. 343 from the mid 1930s. It was listed in a catalog as a 343, 343-2, or 343D to designate the style of decoration. I do not believe the decoration has any influence on the value of this pot.

6-cup pot $30.00

Ribbed Bottom 6-cup variations.

Autumn Leaves

The Autumn Leaves design was used on two distinctive shapes. The first being a vertically ribbed pot with a center band of the leaves. This has been found in two sizes but not in a sugar or creamer yet.

The second shape is a French Drip coffee maker, Catalog No. 333. This shape is also from the mid 1930s and was shown in three variations (333, 333D, and 333-1). I have confirmed three different decorated versions and there may be more.

Ribbed:
4-cup pot $25.00
6-cup pot $30.00

French Drip:
6-cup pot $30.00

Autumn Leaves ribbed 4-cup pot (missing lid) and 6-cup pot.

Daisy Chain

This is a French Drip coffee maker, Catalog No. 333-1 variation from the mid 1930s. It is named for the brown transfer print design depicting a chain of daisies.

6-cup pot $30.00

Daisy Chain French Drip 6-cup pot and Autumn Leaves French Drip 6-cup pot.

Pastel Floral

The Pastel Floral is also a French Drip. It is Catalog No. 333D and is shown in the 1934 catalog in the Reprints section.

6-cup pot $30.00

Pastel Floral French Drip 6-cup pot. Photo courtesy of Pauline (Kobler) Almquist.

French Drip #566

Also from the mid 1930s, this has been found undecorated and in two decorated versions so far. It would not be surprising if others appear. Once again, I do not feel the decoration affects the pricing.

6-cup pot $35.00

French Drip #566 pots in two decorated versions and undecorated.

Cameo Silhouette

The Cameo Silhouette has been found with an ivory or apple green body. Both have a man in black silhouette. The shape is from the mid 1930s and it was a French Drip coffee maker, Catalog No. 556D. Add $10.00 to price for apple green color.

6-cup pot $35.00

Cameo Silhouette 6-cup pot.

Ribbed Betty

This very unusual pot is being named in honor of my best Porcelier pal, Betty Gustafson. She is the only person I know who has this piece. She calls it her "chocolate pot."

I hope that all the Porcelier collectors will give me some leverage on naming this one, as I have completely exhausted my vocabulary in trying to find a descriptive name for this, short of another ribbed variation.

6-cup pot $35.00

Ribbed Betty 6-cup pot.

Solid

The pots classified in this Solid category came in three distinct shapes (tankard, ribbed, and tapered) and two colors (ivory and green). There is a solid electric percolator shown in the Hostess, Platinum, and Percolator Sets section. It is very similar to the tankard shape.

In addition, the tankard shape has just recently been found with the Field Flowers decal. So much for assuming they would only be in solid colors.

Tankard:
6-cup pot (solid) $30.00
6-cup pot (decal) $35.00

Ribbed:
6-cup pot $30.00

Tapered:
6-cup pot $30.00

*Add $5.00 for green color

Solid Tankard 6-cup ivory and 6-cup green pots.

Tankard 6-cup with Field Flowers decal (missing lid).

Solid Ribbed 6-cup pot.

Solid Tapered 6-cup green pot.

Leaves

This is also called "Flames" by some collectors. The background is a faint vertical rib. Around the lower half, there are two rows of what seem to be leaves or flames. They are perpendicular to the bottom, as if they are coming out of the bottom. They are shaded butterscotch, turning into a pale blue as the color gets to the top of the leaves. The lid has the same ribbed background with a layer of leaves radiating from the finial. It is shaded in the same pale blue on the leaves and finial.

Just before going to press, I heard rumors of this being seen in a 4-cup size.

2-cup pot $32.00

Leaves 2-cup pot.

Ocean Waves

This is named for the raised wave-like pattern around the top portion of the pot. The painted flower design varies slightly from piece to piece due to hand decorating.

2-cup pot $32.00

Ocean Waves 2-cup pot.

Diamond Leaf

The body of the Diamond Leaf is a raised pattern of leaves inside diamonds. There is a diamond border at the very rim of the pot and the painted decoration carries out the same theme in blue, green, rust, and brown.

2-cup pot $32.00

Diamond Leaf 2-cup pot.

Sunken Panel

Once again, Porcelier made use of the blue and rust floral design. This time it is in the center vertical panel of the pot, which is also indented giving it a sunken look. The finial is an arch shape.

2-cup pot $32.00

Sunken panel 2-cup pot.

107

Hedge Row

The body of this pot looks almost like rows of bricks or building blocks. The raised grass or vegetation-like pattern above it resembles the top of a hedge. Hence Hedge Row. It also makes use of the standard blue and rust floral design in its center.

2-cup pot $32.00

Hedge Row 2-cup pot.

Floral Rope

This 2-cup piece is decorated with an embossed pattern of blue flowers and butterscotch leaves winding their way around the middle of the pitcher. There is a rope border around the top in the same butterscotch color.

2-cup pitcher $25.00

Floral Rope 2-cup pitcher.

Ribbed Band

This pitcher has vertical ribs around the upper portion and the same floral decoration found on the Basketweave Floral pieces in the center of the body.

2-cup pitcher $25.00

Ribbed Band 2-cup pitcher.

Leaf Band

The basic body of this piece has a raised vertical rib design. Around the center is a row of leaves which are tinted in tan and green. The top and bottom has a painted line as is found on many Porcelier pieces, except that, these are green rather than the usual brown.

2-cup pitcher $25.00

Leaf Band 2-cup pitcher.

Miscellaneous

These items just didn't seem to fit in any other category or pattern. This category encompasses everything from the expected utility ware to the totally surprising fireplace andirons.

Sprig Boiler

This is a double boiler. It originally came with an aluminum bottom which it fit into. The bottoms were separated from these pieces quite easily as they generally were stored in a cupboard with the pans while the china piece was put in a different cupboard. Porcelier bought the bottoms from an outside vendor.

6-cup boiler $30.00

Sprig Boiler without pan.

Quilted Floral Cameo

This very different looking piece is a decanter. I have not seen an original stopper and past employees could not recall if it was china or cork. It is speculated that there were small glasses to go with this to make up a liqueur set.

Decanter $40.00

Quilted Floral Cameo decanter.

Ringed Liqueur Set

This is the most unique set I have seen. It is marked with a Porcelier backstamp on the decanter but not on the glasses. The glasses are similar to a tall shot glass in size.

Seven-piece set $75.00

Ringed Liqueur Set.

Ringed Beer Set

The beer set included a pitcher and six ringed mugs. It was made in both ivory and with multicolored rings, as in the Ringed Liqueur Set. Unfortunately, when I took pictures of the colored pieces they did not turn out. The mugs are the same shape as the ivory mug shown. The pitcher is in the same ring design with a pouring spout but no ice-lip.

Beer pitcher (solid) (not shown) $50.00
Beer pitcher (colored) (not shown) 65.00
Mug (solid) 20.00
Mug (colored) (not shown) 30.00
Seven-piece set (not shown) . . . .185.00 – 260.00

Ringed Beer Mug in ivory.

Wildlife Mugs

This set includes four mugs with a different scene on each. They are a pheasant, a sailfish, a hunting dog, and a horse head. They are not marked and can be found with or without gold trim.

In addition, Porcelier made these same mug shapes as dresser lamps. The top is solid except for the hole in the center to run the wiring through. They were unavailable for photographing.

Mug, each $25.00
Mug, gold trim, each 35.00
Set of four, in original box . . . . .150.00 – 190.00

Set of four Wildlife Mugs with gold trim.

Wildlife Mug Set with gold trim and original box.

Water Pitchers

I have not named the water pitchers. They are referred to by the decal names. It is not known how many different patterns were made. The only two found to date are the Field Flowers and Flower Pot designs. They are unmarked and the bottom is completely flat like the beverage coolers. They have, however been verified through past employees of Porcelier.

Water pitcher $55.00

Water Pitcher with Field Flowers decal.

Water Pitcher with Flower Pot decal.

Spaghetti Bowl

I had previously shown a spaghetti bowl in the Basketweave Wild Flowers pattern under the Matched Appliance Sets. It had the Wild Flower decal and I have since seen this with a third floral decal (even though I was unable to photograph it at the time). I do not know how many different decals were used on these but they are marked with an ink stamp. Many past employees were given a spaghetti bowl as a Christmas gift and several of them remember these being for resale. The decal on the bowl pictured below matches several of the lighting fixtures.

Spaghetti bowl $85.00

Spaghetti Bowl with floral decal.

Salt & Pepper Shakers

Besides the Barock-Colonial, Serv-All, and Oriental Deco shakers there were sets made in designs which did not match other pieces. The two shown are only an example. I have been told that they were decorated in many different ways in this particular shape. Note that below the handle "SALT" or "PEPPER" is embossed.

Set of two shakers . . . .$20.00 – 25.00

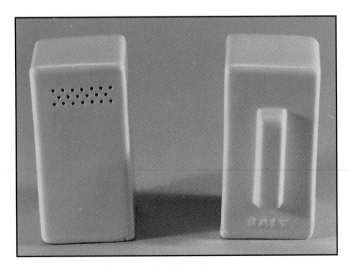

Undecorated salt and pepper set.

Hand-painted salt and pepper set.

Covered Casserole

This casserole has a much more yellow tint than is normally associated with Porcelier. The bottom has an ink backstamp. I have only seen two of these and they were both this same 8½" diameter.

Covered casserole $30.00

Covered Casserole dish.

U.S. Department of Defense Ware

During World War II, Porcelier, along with many other china companies, was commissioned to make ware for the government. These pieces were made to government specifications and are identical to pieces made by the other companies. They may be found carrying backstamps of Hall China, Shenango China, Sterling China, and Homer Laughlin China to name a few.

Items which Porcelier made include cereal bowls, coffee cups, creamers, gravy boats, milk pitchers, mustard jars, sugar bowls, and toothpick holders. They were plain white with a few items carrying a green stripe.

Included in these pictures are cups decorated by employees for their own use. These were not standard issue but are included here only to show the correct shape of the cups made. The pricing is for undecorated pieces. All pieces for standard issue are backstamped with a Porcelier mark. The gravy boat carries a special U.S.Q.M.C. mark as shown here.

Cereal bowl $6.00
Coffee cup 6.00
Cream pitcher .10.00
Gravy boat 25.00
Milk pitcher (not shown) 25.00
Mustard jar (not shown) 12.00
Sugar bowl (not shown) 10.00
Toothpick holder (not shown) 10.00

Coffee cups (decorated).

Gravy boat.

Cereal Bowl.

Bottom mark on gravy boat.

Cream pitcher.

Beverage Coolers

These refrigerator beverage coolers were designed and patented by Emanuel Dym in 1932. A copy of the patent drawing is included in the Reprints section.

To date they have been found in two colors: white and apple green.

Barrel (low) 60.00
Barrel (high) 60.00
Rectangle 75.00

*Add $10.00 each for apple green color

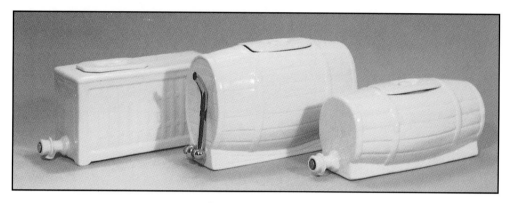

Beverage coolers.

Appliance Coasters

These sturdy coasters were made for use under heavy appliances such as wringer washers, refrigerators, and stoves. I'm not sure, but see no reason they wouldn't have been used under other furniture as well.

They have been found in white and apple green and in two sizes. They have an embossed mark which is shown in the Labels and Marks section. I do not feel that the color makes a difference in the pricing on these pieces.

Set of four, small . . . .$20.00 – 28.00
Set of four, large . . . . .22.00 – 30.00

Appliance coasters.

Towel Bars

The three examples shown are only one style to show the three color variations that have been found. Another style is pictured in the Lighting Fixtures section among a grouping of electrical/utility type pieces.

Set of two . . . .$12.00 – 15.00

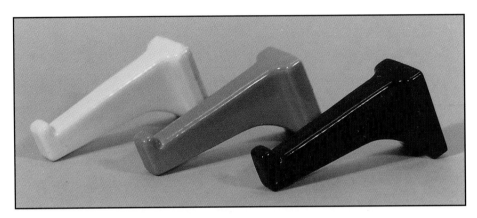

Towel bars.

Fireplace Andirons

These were made in the early to mid 1940s for a very short time as they were not a popular seller. They were made in sections and held together by a rod which runs through the center and bolts to the metal andiron stands. They are 23" high.

Set of two . . . .$250.00 – 325.00

Fireplace andirons.

Powder Jar

This piece was made by the Porcelier Company and was given to employees as a Christmas gift. It is unmarked. I am not positive if they ever made these for resale. Since it was a company approved piece, I have chosen to include it here rather than in the Novelty Section.

Powder jar . . . .$70.00 – 85.00

Powder jar.

Advertising Piece

This cute little double pot is just under 4" in height and is one piece. It is a miniature copy of the Colonial pattern and says "Porcelier Mfg. Co. Greensburg PA" on the front. The back reads "Vitrified China Drip Coffee Maker."

It was made to be given out as an advertising piece although some past employees remember getting one as a gift.

Advertising piece . . . .$175.00 – 200.00

Advertising piece front view.
"PORCELIER MFG. CO. GREENSBURG PA."

Advertising piece back view.
"VITRIFIED CHINA DRIP COFFEE MAKER."

Dual Company Pieces

The patterns shown here have been conclusively proven to be made by Porcelier and sold under both the Porcelier label and another company label.

Other pieces pictured elsewhere found with two different marks include the appliances in the Serv-All and Colonial Silhouette patterns. They have been found with either Porcelier or Heatmaster marks. In addition, many of the lighting fixtures carry both Porcelier marks and Harmony House labels.

I am only including proven pieces, even though I have suspicions about other items.

Porcelier/De-Luxe

This upper ribbed pot was made for both Porcelier and De-luxe Sales Company, Inc. of New York. The brown transfer design has been found marked with either or both marks. There is a light fixture with the same brown transfer design in the Lighting Fixtures section.

The flower design has only been found with the Porcelier backstamp.

<blockquote>
6-cup pot, brown design $30.00
6-cup pot, floral design 40.00
</blockquote>

Left: 6-cup pot marked "Porcelier."
Right: 6-cup pot with dripper marked "De-luxe Sales Co., Inc."

6-cup pot with floral decals marked "Porcelier."

Porcelier/Sears

This Cattail pot was made for both Porcelier and Sears, Roebuck & Company. The Porcelier pot has orange cattails while the Sears version has ochre ones. They have been found with either red or black enamel drippers.

The Sears backstamp is shown in the Label and Marks section. Note that this particular mark reads "Vitrified China" above the cattails rather than "Oven Proof," which appears on pieces made for Sears by Universal Potteries.

In 1942 Sears sold this pot for $1.75 with a red enamel dripper. They also advertised that it made 7 cups of coffee or 9 cups of tea.

7-cup pot $35.00
7-cup pot w/original enamel dripper 60.00

Left: 7-cup cattail pot marked "Porcelier."
Right: 7-cup Cattail pot marked "Sears, Roebuck & Co."

Porcelier/Hankscraft

This egg cooker and egg cup set is in the same design as the platinum percolator sets. Porcelier's is unmarked while the pieces made for Hankscraft are all marked, including the egg cups. I have included pictures for comparison of the minute variations in these two sets. Note that the Porcelier egg cups are a fraction taller, a fraction wider in diameter, but the platinum stripes stand out more on the Hankscraft pieces.

Egg cup (each) . . . .$8.00 – 10.00
Electric egg cooker 35.00

Egg cooker and egg cup set marked "Porcelier" (egg cups not marked).

Hankscraft egg cup with black trim.

Left: Porcelier egg cup.
Right: Hankscraft egg cup.

Left: Bottom of Porcelier egg cup.
Right: Bottom of Hankscraft egg cup.

Novelty Items

This category is indeed a special category. It includes the items which were made by past employees on their breaks and otherwise. Many of these items were specially made as gifts. Some of them are unauthorized copies of other potters' pieces. These were generally called "government ware" by past employees and I met very few who did not know what this term referred to. The pieces are not marked as they were not legitimate Porcelier pieces. Most of them are owned by the past employees or their family members.

One interesting thing to note is that there really never was a "one-of-a-kind" item made at Porcelier, with the exception of a person's name being painted onto it. It was an accepted fact that if you made a special piece, you had better make at least a dozen, so that by the time it went through all the steps of production at least one would make it back to you. It seems that if it was a cute item you would have to be sure each person who had to handle it was able to have one too!

Because of the nature of these items, I have not even attempted to put a value on them.

Marbleized Percolator

This most interesting piece really is Porcelier. The Platinum shape gives it away but I do not believe it was decorated in this manner for resale. I think this was decorated by an employee during his or her free time.

Flight

The two special pieces shown here were not made for resale, but rather employee-made pieces. The plaque was made by the men in the clay department, in 1939, and it is the same size as the front of the Flight disc pitcher. I have seen two of these and they belong to past employees. The small bowl is as if the top of the sugar bowl had been cut off an inch and the handles not applied. This belongs to a past employee's family.

Flight wall plaque.

Flight small bowl.

Other Miscellaneous Novelty Items

Ilene baby plate.

Jimmie baby plate.

Baby plate, not personalized.

Decorated bowl.

Janet baby cup, front and side views.

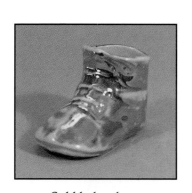

Gold baby shoe.

Toothpick barrel.

Necklace pendant.

Egg baby figurines, front and back.

Cowboy hat ashtray.

Sailor bank thought to be made for
Seaman's Bank of New York, similar
to bank made by McCoy.

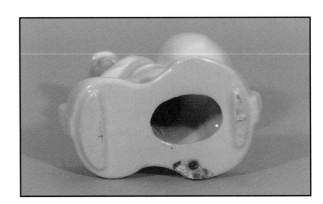

Bottom of Sailor bank.

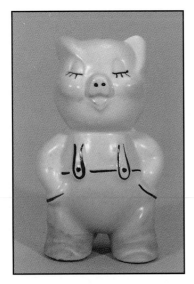

Piggy bank.

Pig figurine.

Pig figurines, front and back.

Deer figurine.

Fawn figurines, front and back.

Lamb figurine.

Squirrel figurine.

Elephant figurine.

Elephant figurine.

Elephant lamp.

Donkey figurines, front and back.

Variously decorated horse figurines.

Horse figurine.

Variously decorated puppy figurines.

Puppy figurine.

Puppy figurines.

Puppy bookends.

Variously decorated matador and bull figurines.

Bear figurine.   Small basket.

Candy or mint dish.

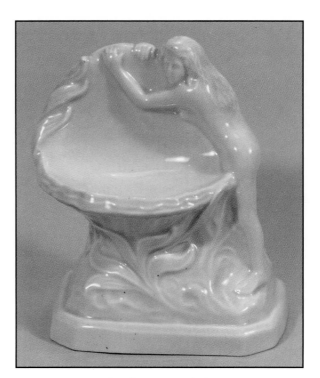

Candy or mint dish.

Cat face dish.

Lady mint dish.

Various ashtrays.

More ashtrays.

Planter or ice bucket? The gentleman who owns this could not remember exactly what its original purpose was.

Candleholder pair with prisms.

Oriental figurine.

Aladdin lamp.

1945 Christmas pot made by Carl Kobler. Photo courtesy of Carol (Kobler) McLaughlin.

Reproductions and Takeoffs

I am including this short section to alert collectors and dealers alike that there are copies out there. They are generally decorated poorly, in the wrong colors, and are slightly larger than originals. The bottom is not usually the Porcelier shape and they are easily detected as fakes. *See the picture below.*

To date I have seen copies and takeoffs of the Hearth, Nautical, Barock-Colonial, and the Double Floral patterns. Some of the shakers and canisters are marked "Japan." The coffee and teapots are not marked.

Dealers need to be especially careful not to mismark these as Porcelier items. I have had friends excitedly bring me pieces from their travels, only to find they are fakes. Unfortunately, the dealer tags on the pieces said Porcelier, the prices reflected that of Porcelier, and my friends did not know, as they are not collectors.

Barock-Colonial Copies

These shakers, in several other color combinations such as ivory/blue, blue/gold, and ivory/black, have been spotted in a lot of different states. The single range shaker below is a copy marked "Japan." The boxed set, which I consider a take-off type product, is a Napco set.

Nautical Copies

These 2- and 6-cup pots are not marked but, it is very obvious to the experienced collector that, these are not Porcelier quality. I have also seen them in other color combinations. An example of the bottom is shown with the Hearth copies.

Hearth Copies

The canister set is the shape usually made by Purinton and is marked "Made in USA" with a brown ink stamp. It is uncertain if Purinton is the maker or not.

The sugar and 2-cup pot are the only sizes I have seen copies of in the Hearth pattern. It is interesting to note that the lid on the 2-cup pot is actually a copy of the Nautical lid with buoy finial. The smaller picture below the pot is a picture of its bottom.

Lighting Fixtures

These examples are but a brief statement on the versatility with which Porcelier operated. Included in the category of lighting fixtures are single, double, and triple ceiling fixtures; wall sconces; table lamps; chandeliers; and drop lights. They were made for commercial, residential, and industrial use.

In the past three years, there has been a lot of interest in this era of lighting fixture. I have seen some prices soar from $10 each to $100 each (rewired). It seems that the colored fixtures (orchid, black, green, and blue) demand the highest prices.

Porcelier made all their own parts including the metal pieces. They bought the globes mainly from Beaumont Glass of Texas. They were made plain, embossed, and decaled in white, ivory, and colors.

It would be impossible to put names on this multitude of light fixtures and I am not certain that very many people who collect them would appreciate names. Therefore, I have decided to picture them and make any appropriate comments or mention if they match a particular kitchenware pattern. More patterns are shown in the Reprints section.

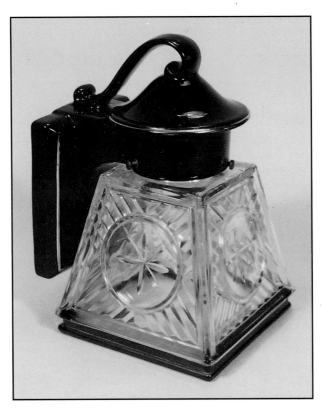

Black outdoor porch light with original glass globe, $80.00.

Lamps, Chandeliers, and Drop Lights

Originally a chandelier body from 1943 (#9216) and now made into a table lamp (UND).

Table lamp, $70.00.

Small dresser lamp (not on its original base), $15.00.

Table lamp, Antique Rose decal, $45.00.

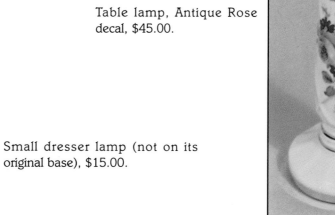

Dutch Boy dresser lamp, $55.00.
A matching Dutch Girl lamp also exists.

Cobblestone dresser lamp, $50.00.

Basketweave dresser lamps, $55.00 each.

Rose table lamp (possible original shade), $55.00.

Rose chandelier, $65.00.

Green and gold drop light, $60.00.

Deco drop light, original globe, $78.00.

Arrow dresser lamp, $60.00.

Table lamp with Antique Rose decal, $70.00.

Various lamp bodies (UND).

Ceiling and Wall Fixtures

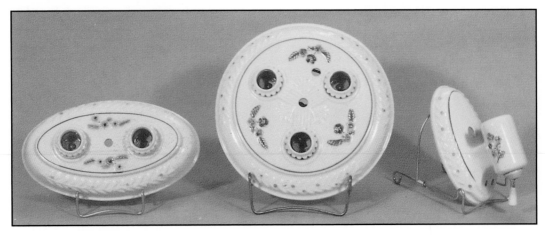

Double ceiling, $35.00; triple ceiling, $55.00; and wall sconce, $35.00.

Single ceiling fixture, $30.00.

Triple ceiling fixture, $55.00.

Wall sconce, $35.00.

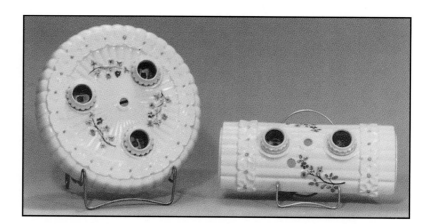

Triple ceiling fixture, $55.00; and double ceiling fixture, $40.00.

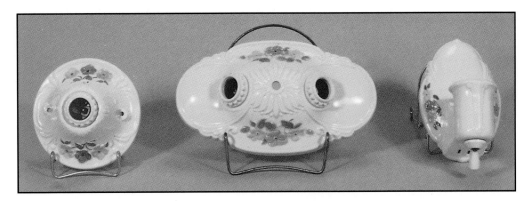

Single ceiling, $30.00; double ceiling, $35.00; and wall sconce, $35.00.

Barock-Colonial wall sconces, $40.00 each; and double ceiling fixture, $55.00.

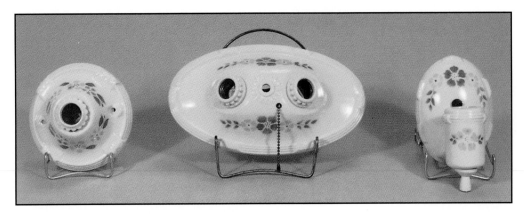

Single ceiling, $30.00; double ceiling, $35.00; and wall sconce, $35.00 (sold by Montgomery Wards in 1948 for $1.45, $2.39, and $1.75).

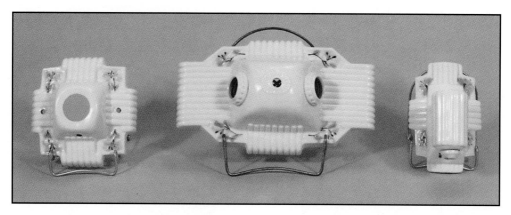

Single ceiling, $30.00; double ceiling, $35.00; and wall sconce, $35.00. (Sears Fostoria 1939 – 1940, priced at $.79, $.94, and $.98.)

Triple ceiling fixture, $60.00.

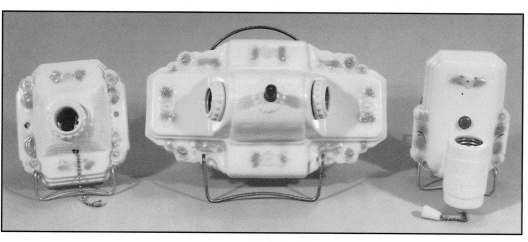

Basketweave single ceiling, $35.00; double ceiling, $60.00; and wall sconce, $35.00 (Montgomery Wards 1942 – 1943, original costs $1.00, $1.35, and $1.25).

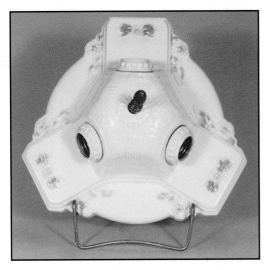

Basketweave triple ceiling fixture, $75.00 (Montgomery Wards 1942 – 1943, original cost of $1.85).

Triple ceiling fixture, $60.00.

Single ceiling fixture, $40.00.

Double ceiling fixture, $35.00, from 1943.

Double ceiling fixture, $30.00, from 1943.

Single ceiling fixture, $30.00; and wall sconce, $35.00 (from 1943 catalog numbers 5001-10 and 5026-10).

Wall sconce with original shade, $47.00. (These decals match the spaghetti bowl shown in the Miscellaneous section.)

Double ceiling fixture, $45.00; and wall sconces, $40.00 each. (In 1942 Wards sold these for $1.75 or $1.45 in Blue or Dusty Coral.)

Single ceiling fixture, $40.00 (in 1942 Wards sold for $1.25).

Wall sconce with original shade, $48.00.

Wall fixture with original shade, $40.00.

146

Triple ceiling fixture, $35.00; and wall sconce, $35.00 (sconce is from 1943 catalog number 646-10 in yellow, blue, or rose).

Single ceiling fixture with original yellow shade, $55.00.

Single ceiling fixture with original pink shade, $55.00.

Wall sconce, $35.00.

Single ceiling fixture, $35.00.

Double ceiling fixture, $50.00.

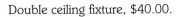

Double ceiling fixture, $40.00.

Wall sconce, $35.00.

Ceiling plate for chandelier (UND) and single ceiling fixture, $30.00.

Triple ceiling, $65.00; and double ceiling, $50.00 fixtures.

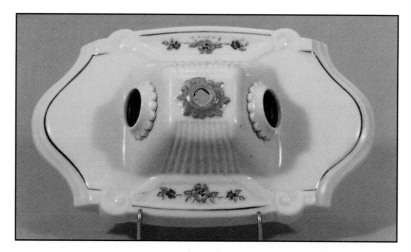

Double ceiling fixture, $35.00.

Double ceiling fixture, $40.00; and wall sconce, $35.00.

Single ceiling fixture, $25.00.

Wall sconce, $35.00.

Single ceiling fixture, $25.00.

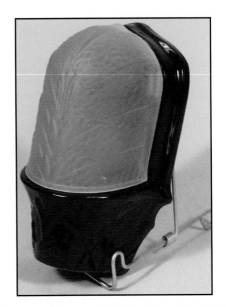

Single wall sconce, $80.00 with original globe
(1931 design by George Wilson).

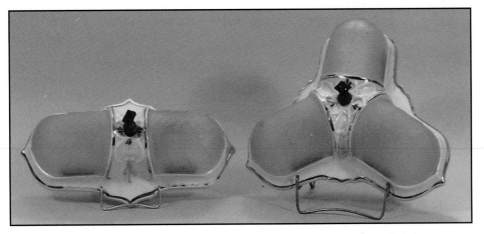

Double, $75.00; and triple, $90.00 ceiling fixtures with original globes
(1931 design by George Wilson).

150

Double ceiling fixture, $40.00.

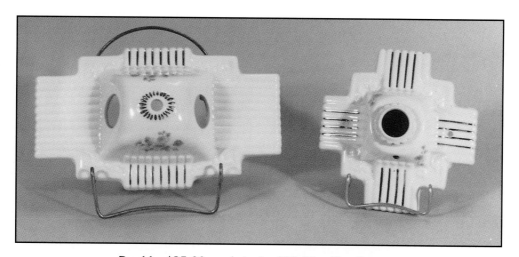

Double, $35.00; and single, $30.00 ceiling fixtures.

Double ceiling fixture, $30.00.

Double ceiling fixture, $45.00.

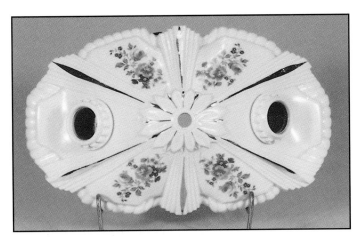

Double ceiling fixture, $40.00.

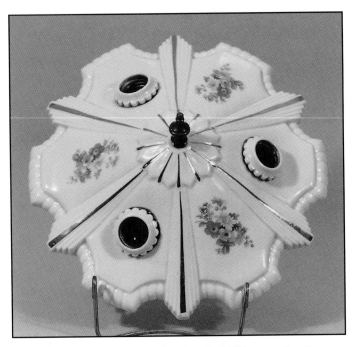

Triple ceiling fixture, $60.00, Field Flowers decal.

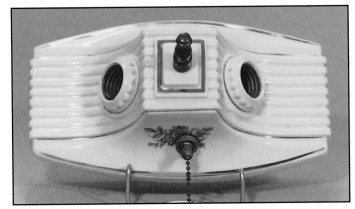

Double ceiling fixture, $35.00.

Double ceiling fixture, $50.00 (1930 design by Hyman Tauber).

Single ceiling fixture, $30.00.

Single ceiling fixture, $30.00.

Wall sconce, $45.00.

Wall sconce, $35.00.

Wall sconce, $35.00. Matches Porcelier/De-luxe pattern in Dual Company section.

Wall sconce, $25.00.

Triple ceiling fixture and shade Horse & Saddle Design from 1943 catalog number 2814, $145.00.

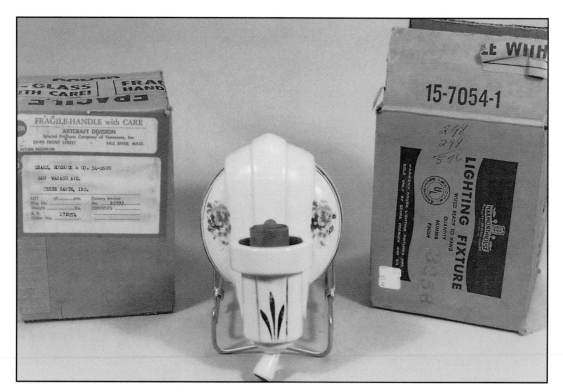

Single wall sconce, $35.00. Shown with original shipping cartons from Sears and Harmony House.

Triple ceiling fixture Six-Shooter & Steer Design from 1943 & 1951 catalog number 4714, $110.00.

Single ceiling fixture, $25.00, from 1951.

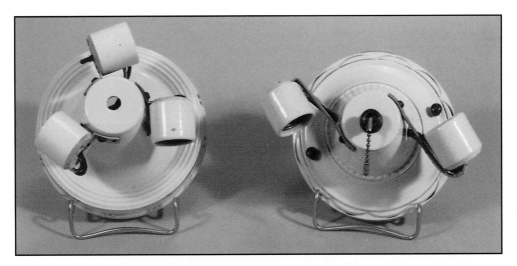

Triple ceiling, $20.00; and double ceiling fixtures, $20.00.

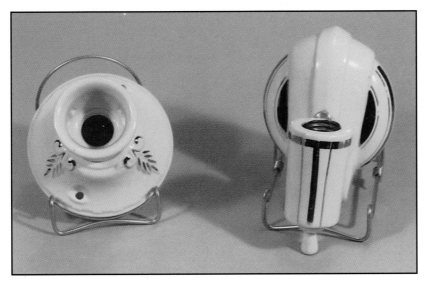

Single ceiling fixture, $20.00; and wall sconce, $20.00; from 1942.

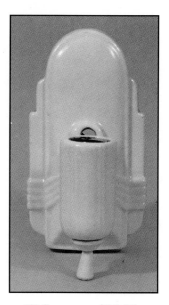

Single wall fixtures: white, $20.00; green, $25.00. (White fixture is a 1931 Hyman Tauber design.)

Wall sconce, $15.00.

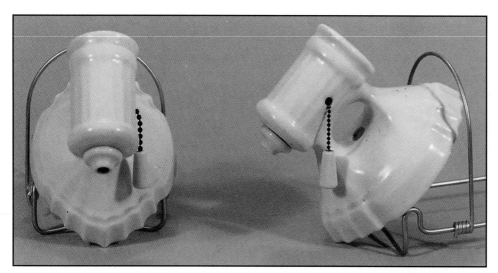

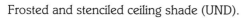

Wall sconces (front and side views), $20.00 each

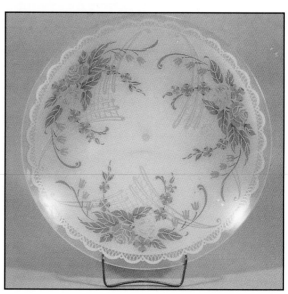

Frosted and stenciled ceiling shade (UND).

Frosted ceiling shade (UND).

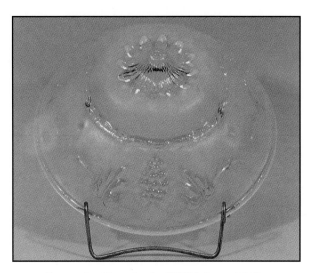

Frosted ceiling shade (UND) from 1943.

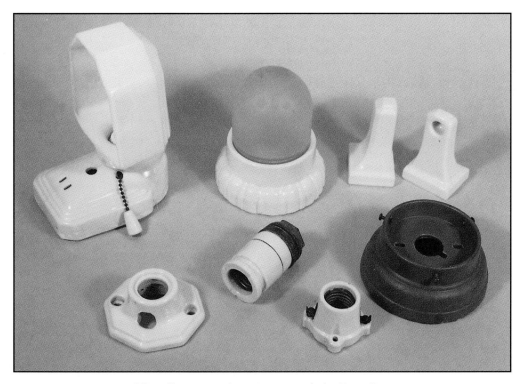

Miscellaneous other pieces made by Porcelier.

Reprints

In this section I am including reprints of anything I felt would be of general interest to Porcelier collectors. As for the reprints of patents and designs, I have only reprinted the drawings filed in connection with those items. I have deliberately left out the text portions of the patents.

Porcelier Company Catalogs

Porcelier Matched Appliances, catalog no. 15, 1934. Courtesy of Jim Barker.

Porcelier Manufacturing Co.

MANUFACTURERS OF

VITRIFIED PORCELAIN

PORCELIER LIGHTING EQUIPMENT
AND WIRING DEVICES

PORCELIER MATCHED
ELECTRICAL APPLIANCES

Greensburg, Pa.

September 25, 1934.

Gentlemen:

The inclosed catalogue fully illustrates and describes our "Matched Appliances", which we have successfully developed after years of research.

These appliances are NEW--DIFFERENT--SMART, with attractive decorations--rich pastel ivory body and chrome plated fittings.

"Matched Appliances" are popularly priced and within reach of everybody as you will note from the attached price list. Every housewife will want to own a set.

We will welcome an opportunity to serve you, and remain,

Very truly yours,

PORCELIER MANUFACTURING COMPANY,

E. DYM:RE
Incl.

PORCELIER MANUFACTURING COMPANY

Greensburg, Pennsylvania

SEPTEMBER 25, 1934.

PRICE LIST

Catalogue No.	Description	Net Price
	ELECTRIC APPLIANCES	
410	Percolator Set with Sugar & Creamer, Decorated	$3.95
210	Urn Set with Sugar & Creamer, Decorated	5.00
810	Percolator Set with Sugar & Creamer, Decorated	2.85
910	Urn Set with Sugar & Creamer, Decorated	4.00
2007	Colonial Percolator Set with Sugar & Creamer, Decorated	4.50
2009	Colonial Urn Set with Sugar & Creamer, Decorated	6.00
3007	Modern Perc. Set with Sugar & Creamer, Decorated	3.95
3009	Modern Urn Set with Sugar & Creamer, Decorated	5.00
710	Perc. Set with Sugar & Creamer, Decorated	2.85
*450	Set, Non-Automatic Waffle Iron with Batter Pitcher & Syrup Jar	5.25
450	Non-Automatic Waffle Iron Only, Decorated	3.85
*451	Set, Automatic Waffle Iron with Batter Pitcher & Syrup Jar Dec.	5.65
451	Automatic Waffle Iron only, Decorated	4.30
*460	Set, Non-Automatic Waffle Iron with Batter Pitcher & Syrup Jar	5.25
460	Non-Automatic Waffle Iron only, Decorated	3.85
*461	Set, Automatic Waffle Iron with Batter Pitcher & Syrup Jar Dec.	5.65
461	Automatic Waffle Iron, only Decorated	4.30
2002	Colonial Toaster, Decorated	5.25
3002	Modern Toaster, Decorated	5.25
2004	Colonial Sandwich Toaster & Grill, Decorated	4.75
3004	Modern Sandwich Toaster & Grill, Decorated	4.75
2010	Colonial Casserole, Decorated	.90
3010	Modern Casserole, Decorated	.90
2015	Colonial Cookie Jar, Decorated	1.10
3015	Modern Cookie Jar, Decorated	1.10
2011	Colonial Tea Pot, Decorated	.65
2011	Undecorated Colonial Tea Pot	.50
3011	Modern Tea Pot, Decorated	.65
3011	Undecorated Modern Tea Pot	.50
2016	Colonial 4-Piece Utility Set, Decorated	1.80
3016	Modern 4-Piece Utility Set, Decorated	1.80
2020	Colonial 4-Piece Kitchen Shaker Set	.80
3020	Modern 4-Piece Kitchen Shaker Set	.80
2012	Colonial Syrup Jar, Decorated	.55
3012	Modern Syrup Jar, Decorated	.55
2014	Colonial Batter Pitcher, Decorated	.82½
3014	Modern Batter Pitcher, Decorated	.82½

(*) Indicates Waffle Sets

PORCELIER   MANUFACTURING   COMPANY

Greensburg, Pennsylvania.

September 25, 1934.

PRICE LIST

Catalogue No.	Description	Net Price
410	Sugar & Creamer Set only, Decorated — — — —	$ .85
210	Sugar & Creamer Set Only, Decorated — — — —	.85
810	Sugar & Creamer Set Only, Decorated — — — —	.85
910	Sugar & Creamer Set Only, Decorated — — — —	.85
2007	Colonial Sugar & Creamer Set Only, Decorated — — —	1.00
2009	Colonial Sugar & Creamer Set Only, Decorated — — —	1.00
3007	Modern Sugar & Creamer Set Only, Decorated — — —	.85
3009	Modern Sugar & Creamer Set Only, Decorated — — —	.85

FRENCH DRIP COFFEE MAKERS

333	Ivory or Green — — — — — — — —	.65
333D	Decorated on Ivory — — — — — — — —	.90
343	Ivory or Green — — — — — — — —	.65
343D	Decorated on Ivory — — — — — — — —	.90
576	Ivory — — — — — — — —	.85
576	Ivory with Sugar & Creamer — — — — — —	1.45
576D	Decorated — — — — — — —	1.10
576D	Decorated, with Sugar & Creamer — — — — —	1.95
556	Ivory or Green — — — — — — —	.70
556D	Decorated — — — — — — —	.95
566	Underglazed Decoration — — — — — — —	.65
566D	Decorated — — — — — — —	.95
333-1	Underglazed Decoration — — — — — —	.65
343-2	Underglazed Decoration — — — — — —	.65
754	Water Cooler — — — — — — —	.75

TRAYS

500	Chrome. Modern Tray — — — — — — —	1.00
1000	Chrome Tray — — — — — — —	1.00
2611	Composition Ivory and Black Tray — — — —	1.00

TERMS: 2% 10 Days, E.O.M. Net 30 Days.

F.O.B. Greensburg, Pa.

IN MATCHED APPLIANCES BY PORCELIER, the trade is able to offer for the first time, a harmonized line of household ware, both electric and non-electric, which has an instant appeal to the woman of the home.

These pieces, matched in material and design are made of the highest grade of vitrified china. They are practical for use in any kitchen—attractive in any dining-room. Already smart merchandisers throughout the country have acclaimed this line the outstanding leader in the "parade of new products."

MATCHED APPLIANCES BY PORCELIER are new—different —smart. Even though each piece is perfect in itself—and can be sold on its own merits, the complete line gives a chance to build up larger sales, and offers real inducement to the buyer to replace outmoded equipment.

We present, first »»»

THE SERV-ALL LINE

styled in simplicity...with moulded relief motif, accentuated by red and black inlay striping or a choice of platinum.

* * *

PORCELIER MANUFACTURING COMPANY... GREENSBURG, PA.

* * *

No. 3009

Serv-All Electric Urn Set

A beautiful companion to the finest tableware. A bright, gleaming surface that is made of ivory tint vitrified china with molded relief decoration in either platinum or red and black inlaid lines. Chromium faucet with black handles. Latest type of electric heating element, listed as standard by Underwriters' Laboratories. Sets consisting of 3-pieces, a 9 cup urn with sugar and creamer to match are packed in individual shipping containers, including cord set. Weight 11 lbs.

MATCHED APPLIANCES *by Porcelier*
• 2 •

No. 3007

Serv-All Electric Percolator Set

The ultra modern lines . . . . the rare charm and simplicity make this the outstanding of the latest creations in percolators. Similar to the urn, it is made of ivory tint vitrified china, and decorated with either platinum or red and black inlaid lines. The sugar and creamer harmoniously carry out the design and complete the set. The set consists of 3-pieces, a 7-cup percolator, sugar and creamer and comes packed in individual shipping container, including cord set. Weight 10 lbs.

MATCHED APPLIANCES *by Porcelier*
• 3 •

No. 3002

HOW IT WORKS

Place bread in slots. Press down lever to start. When switch clicks, bread is toasted. Lift lever and up comes the toast. Can be adjusted to light, medium or dark. Not necessary to pre-heat toaster.

Serv-All Automatic 2 Slice Toaster

The final word in modern design and beauty as well as utility. Toasts both sides of two slices of bread at the same time. Insulated to retain heat, as proven by tests which shows element to remain warm thirty minutes after using. Has heat regulator and is automatic. Made of vitrified china. Decorated to match other modern appliances in either platinum or red and black. Packed in individual container, including cord set. Weight 8 lbs.

MATCHED APPLIANCES *by Porcelier*
• 4 •

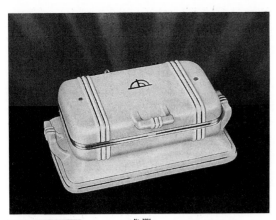

No. 3004

Serv-All Electric Sandwich Toaster and Grill

Provides for toasting two large, delicious sandwiches at a time.

When frying bacon and eggs, etc., our special grid design permits butter or fat to drain into a provided receptacle from both grids.

The set that becomes indispensable the moment it is bought. Not only does it make delicious toasted sandwiches but has extra uses as depicted by the artist sketches at left. Both grids are designed to allow butter or fat to drain into a special receptacle furnished with each set. Made of vitrified china with decoration to match the other appliances in the line. Packed in individual shipping container, including cord set. Weight 10 lbs.

MATCHED APPLIANCES *by Porcelier*

·5·

No. 451

Serv-All Vitrified China Automatic Waffle Iron

No. 450 Non-Automatic

The latest design grids with tested and approved heating element bakes evenly over entire surface and assures evenly browned waffles.

An entirely new creation, this vitrified china Waffle Iron "has everything" including, besides a heat regulator the "Red Eye" signal light, which removes the guesswork and assures the making of perfect waffles. Decoration can be had in platinum or red and black. The batter jug and syrup jar to match make up the set and gives added sales appeal. Waffle iron can be had without batter jug and syrup jar. Sets come packed in individual shipping container, including cord set. Weight 10 lbs.

No. 3012 Syrup Jar   No. 3014 Batter Pitcher
Weight 6 lbs.

·6· MATCHED APPLIANCES *by Porcelier*

No. 3020

Serv-All Shaker Set

A beautiful new design in vitrified china. Easy to keep clean. Almost unbreakable. A handy range set for cooking. Decorated to match the "Serv-All Line" in platinum or red and black. Set consists of 1 salt, 1 pepper, 1 sugar and 1 flour. Packed set to a carton. 6 sets to shipping container. Weight 21 lbs.

Serv-All Casserole Combination

Made of vitrified china. Heat-proof for baking. Has an added utility feature as the cover serves as a pie baker when used separately. The "Modern" relief pattern and decoration in platinum or red and black adds smartness when serving at mealtime. Packed individually 12 to carton. Weight 57 lbs.

No. 3010

Serv-All Tea Pot

Made of vitrified china. Makes 1 to 5 cups of tea. Matches the "Serv-All" design and decoration in platinum or red and black. Packed individually, 12 to carton. Weight 33 lbs.

No. 3011

COOKIES

No. 3015

Serv-All Cookie Jar

Made of vitrified china. A storage jar for cookies, pretzels, etc. Preserves freshness longer. Matches the "Serv-All" design and decoration in platinum or red and black. Packed individually, 6 to carton. Weight 35 lbs.

TEA   COFFEE   SUGAR   SALT

No. 3016

Serv-All Utility Set

Made of vitrified china. Easy to keep clean. Sturdy with ideal capacity. A kitchen utility set that matches the "Serv-All Line" of appliances decorated in platinum or red and black. Set consists of 1 tea, 1 coffee, 1 sugar, 1 salt. Packed set to a carton. 6 sets to shipping container. Weight 50 lbs.

·7·

We now present ...

THE BAROCK-COLONIAL LINE

A shape and decoration that is distinctive.
Its captivating beauty has outstanding appeal.

* * *

PORCELIER MANUFACTURING COMPANY ... GREENSBURG, PA.

* * *

No. 2009

Barock-Colonial Electric Urn Set

A majestically appearing set that any hostess will surely be proud to own. Made of ivory tint vitrified china with conventional pyramid design and twisted rope effect handles. Decorated in red and gold or gold only. Urn has, in addition, pastel floral decoration. Chromium faucet. Latest type of electric heating element, listed as standard by Underwriters' Laboratories. Sugar and creamer to match are made to harmonize perfectly and complete the set. Sets consisting of 3-pieces, a 9-cup urn, sugar and creamer are packed in individual shipping containers, including cord set. Weight 12 lbs.

MATCHED APPLIANCES *by Porcelier*

• 10 •

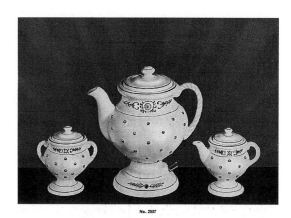

No. 2007

Barock-Colonial Electric Percolator Set

Women who appreciate the unusual will delight in the beauty of this set. Made of vitrified china and decorated in red and gold or gold only similar to the urn. Makes 7 cups of delicious coffee. The sugar and creamer carry out perfectly the graceful beauty of the set. Latest long life heating element listed as standard by Underwriters' Laboratories. Sets consisting of 7-cup percolator, sugar and creamer come packed in individual shipping containers, including cord set. Weight 9 lbs.

MATCHED APPLIANCES *by Porcelier*

• 11 •

HOW IT WORKS

Place bread in slots. Press down lever to start. When switch clicks, bread is toasted. Lift lever and up comes the toast. Can be adjusted to light, medium or dark. Not necessary to pre-heat toaster.

No. 2002

Barock-Colonial Automatic 2 Slice Toaster

A modern toaster with a Colonial design and decoration. Modern . . . . because it toasts both sides of two slices of bread at the same time, and does it better. Its insulation qualities are such that the unit remains warm for a half an hour after using. A heat regulator provides for desired speed in toasting. The automatic feature indicates when toast is ready. Made of vitrified china. Decorated in red and gold or gold only. Packed in individual shipping container, including cord set. Weight 8 lbs.

MATCHED APPLIANCES *by Porcelier*

• 12 •

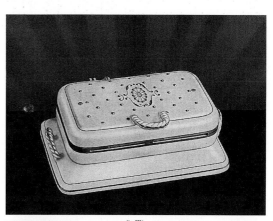

Provides for toasting two large, delicious sandwiches at a time.

When frying bacon and eggs, etc., our special grid design permits butter or fat to drain into a provided receptacle from both grids.

No. 2004

Barock-Colonial Electric Sandwich Toaster and Grill

Not only a clever set that will add distinction to a finely appointed table service but an indispensable utility that makes toasted sandwiches or fries bacon and eggs in a jiffy. Specially designed grids permit butter or fat to drain from both into receptacle that goes with the set. Made of vitrified china. Decorated in red and gold or gold only to match the other "Colonial" appliances. Packed in individual shipping container, including cord set. Weight 10 lbs.

MATCHED APPLIANCES *by Porcelier*

• 13 •

No. 461

Barock-Colonial
Automatic Waffle Iron

No. 460 Non-Automatic

Particularly beautiful in the Colonial decoration is the latest automatic Waffle Set made up of waffle iron, batter jug and syrup jar. The automatic features include not only a heat regulator but the newest "Red Eye" signal which directs the making of perfect waffles. Made of vitrified china and decorated in red and gold or gold only. Enclosed chromium hinge. Easy to clean. Adds distinction to the table service. Set packed in individual shipping containers, including cord set. Weight 10 lbs.

The latest design grids with tested and approved heating element bakes evenly over entire surface and assures evenly browned waffles.

No. 2012 Syrup Jar   No. 2014 Batter Pitcher
Weight 6 lbs.

MATCHED APPLIANCES *by Porcelier*

• 14 •

No. 2029

Barock-Colonial Shaker Set

A beautiful new shape made of vitrified china. Easy to clean. Practically unbreakable. A handy range set for the kitchen. Decorated in red and gold or gold only. Set consists of 1 salt, 1 pepper, 1 sugar and 1 flour. Packed set to carton. Six sets to shipping container. Weight 21 lbs.

Barock-Colonial Casserole Combination

Made of vitrified china. Heat-proof for baking. Has an added utility feature as the cover serves as a pie baker when used separately. The "Colonial" design and decoration in red and gold or gold entirely makes it an ideal dish for serving baked foods. Packed individually. 12 to carton. Weight 57 lbs.

No. 2010

Barock-Colonial Tea Pot

Made of vitrified china. Makes 1 to 5 cups of tea. Matches the "Colonial" design and decoration in red and gold or gold entirely. Packed individually, 12 to carton. Weight 33 lbs.

No. 2011

Barock-Colonial Cookie Jar

Made of vitrified china. A storage jar for cookies, pretzels, etc. Preserves freshness longer. Matches the "Colonial" design and decoration in red and gold or gold entirely. Packed individually 6 to carton. Weight 35 lbs.

No. 2015

Barock-Colonial Utility Set

Made of vitrified china. Easy to keep clean. Sturdy with ideal capacity. A kitchen utility set that matches the "Colonial Line" of appliances. Decorated in red and gold or gold entirely. Set consists of 1 tea, 1 coffee, 1 sugar, 1 salt. Packed set to carton. 6 sets to shipping container. Weight 50 lbs.

No. 2016

• 15 •

No. 333—FRENCH DRIP COFFEE MAKER
Plain, no decoration. Made of vitrified china in ivory or green body furnished with aluminum drip top. Makes 6 cups of delicious coffee. Packed individually, 12 to carton. Weight 48 lbs.

No. 333D—FRENCH DRIP COFFEE MAKER
Decorated with red and black lines and pastel floral design. Vitrified china in ivory tint. Furnished with aluminum drip top. Six cup size. Packed individually, 12 to carton. Weight 48 lbs.

No. 343—FRENCH DRIP COFFEE MAKER
Plain, no decoration. A Colonial shape with moulded corrugation. Vitrified china; ivory or green body. Aluminum drip top. Makes 6 cups of delicious coffee. Packed individually, 12 to carton. Weight 43 lbs.

No. 343D—FRENCH DRIP COFFEE MAKER
Decorated with beautiful pastel floral and red and black lines. Moulded corrugation. Made of vitrified china. Ivory tint body. Aluminum drip top. Six cup size. Packed individually, 12 to carton. Weight 43 lbs.

FRENCH DRIP COFFEE MAKERS *by Porcelier*

• 16 •

No. 576D—DECORATED FRENCH DRIP COFFEE MAKER SET
No. 576—UNDECORATED FRENCH DRIP COFFEE MAKER SET
The latest in the line. Matches the sensational line of "Serv-All" matched appliances. Made of vitrified china with moulded relief lines and platinum or red and black decoration on ivory body. Sugar and creamer to match. Furnished with aluminum drip top. Makes 6 cups of delicious coffee. Packed in individual shipping container. Can be had without sugar and creamer. Weight 9 lbs.

No. 566D—DECORATED FRENCH DRIP COFFEE MAKER
No. 566—UNDECORATED FRENCH DRIP COFFEE MAKER FURNISHED IN IVORY OR GREEN

A new, modern shape Coffee Maker of 6 cup capacity. Made of vitrified china. Decorated with an entirely new colored pastel and red and black lines on ivory body. Aluminum drip top. Packed individually, 12 to carton. Weight 49 lbs.

No. 556D—DECORATED FRENCH DRIP COFFEE MAKER
No. 556—UNDECORATED FRENCH DRIP COFFEE MAKER FURNISHED IN IVORY OR GREEN

Another new, modern shape Coffee Maker of 6 cup capacity. Made of vitrified china in ivory tint. A new series of vertical corrugations and decoration in red and black make it "different". Furnished with aluminum drip top. Packed individually, 12 to carton. Weight 49 lbs.

FRENCH DRIP COFFEE MAKERS *by Porcelier*

• 17 •

No. 333-1—FRENCH DRIP COFFEE MAKER
Beautiful underglazed decoration. Made of vitrified china and furnished complete with aluminum drip top. Makes 6 cups of delicious coffee. Packed individually, 12 to carton. Weight 46 lbs.

No. 343-2—FRENCH DRIP COFFEE MAKER
Attractive underglazed decoration. Vitrified china in ivory tint. Furnished with aluminum drip top. Six cup size. Packed individually, 12 to carton. Weight 43 lbs.

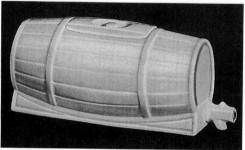

No. 754—U. S. Patent No. 87741
The world's lowest priced vitrified China water and beverage cooler. Increases the efficiency and usefulness of every refrigerator. A compact container 13½" x 5½" x 5¾" for chilling and dispensing water, iced tea, lemonade, root beer and all beverages. Rapid flow faucet is cast in porcelain and equipped with counter-sunk chromium plated push button—the safest and easiest faucet for a refrigerator water cooler. Packed individually, 6 to shipping container. Weight 32 lbs.

· 18 ·

No. 710

Electric Percolator Set

A low priced percolator that has style and eye appeal. An unusual shape with pleasing harmony throughout the set which is made up of 3-pieces, a 7-cup percolator, sugar and creamer. Made of fine, vitrified china of ivory tint body and decorated with pastel floral spray. Has concealed electric heating element, listed as standard by Underwriters' Laboratories. This set is worthy of good display, and, at a price will create many new sales. Packed in individual shipping containers, including cord set. Weight 9 lbs.

ELECTRIC PERCOLATOR SETS *by Porcelier*

· 19 ·

No. 210

Electric Urn Set

A smart, distinctive shape that already has found a welcome in thousands of homes . . . . a proven "good seller." Made of gleaming vitrified china, beautifully decorated with pastel florals and platinum on ivory tinted body. A sugar and creamer that match perfectly and complete the set. Latest type of electric heating element, listed as standard by Underwriters' Laboratories. Chromium leak-proof faucet. Set consists of 3-pieces, a 9 cup urn, 1 sugar and 1 creamer. Packed in individual shipping container, including cord set. Weight 12 lbs.

ELECTRIC URN SETS *by Porcelier*

· 20 ·

No. 410

Electric Percolator Set

A beautifully constructed percolator by Porcelier master craftsmen that blends with the most exquisite of table settings, and also a proven "good seller". Made of vitrified china and decorated with exceptionally beautiful pastels and platinum. The sugar and creamer match perfectly and complete the set. Latest type of electric heating element, listed as standard by Underwriters' Laboratories. Set consists of 3-pieces, a 7-cup percolator, one sugar and one creamer and comes packed in individual shipping container, including cord set. Weight 9 lbs.

ELECTRIC PERCOLATOR SETS *by Porcelier*

· 21 ·

The HOSTESS COFFEE MAKER SET

∾

No. 910
9-Cup

A beautiful modern style delicately decorated with dainty pastel floral design on front panel, also on base. Vitrified China body of rich Old Ivory tint neatly corrugated, which produces a new high light effect. Chromium faucet with black handle. Concealed electric heating element listed as standard by Board of Underwriters.

Imagine the captivating display you can make with this newest of new coffee makers. Weight 12 lbs.

Created by Porcelier

THE SUGAR and CREAM

Every detail of the design, even to the exact contour of the handles is carried out in these perfectly harmonizing accessories. The set complete should be sold as a unit, however, it is quite possible to sell the cream and sugar separate.

THE TRAY

Harmonizes perfectly in design and color treatment. No set would be complete without this tray. Besides the tray is liquor proof and can be used perfectly for serving cocktails. Weight 2½ lbs.

THE URN

Plenty of eye appeal and just as practical in service as it is good looking. China has the very highest rating as a coffee making material. Coffee basket inside insures clear ground-proof coffee of most pleasing flavor.

.. ..

ELECTRIC URN SETS *by Porcelier*

· 22 ·

Created by Porcelier

No. 810

Electric Percolator Set

The set that represents real class in coffee service. Of 7 cup capacity, it stands head and shoulders above everything else in the percolator line. Vitrified china body in rich, old ivory with delicate pastel floral design. Concealed electric heating element listed as standard by Board of Underwriters. Furnished complete with Coffee basket and electric cord and plugs ready for instant use. The sugar and creamer match perfectly. The tray, which is liquor proof, makes a perfect cocktail service and can be included in set. Packed in individual shipping containers, including cord set. Weight 9 lbs.

ELECTRIC PERCOLATOR SETS *by Porcelier*

· 23 ·

No. 500
A modern tray for the Serv-All Line

Simplicity of design with a maximum of area, makes this an ideal tray to sell with the "Serv-All" Urn and Percolator Sets. We also recommend it for the 210, 410 and 710 Sets. It has the highest finish obtainable in chromium plate. It will not discolor or stain and is easy to clean. Its permanency will add sales appeal. Carefully wrapped and faced with tissue to protect the surface and packed in individual containers. Weight 3 lbs.

No. 1000
A special tray for the Colonial Line

An entirely new design, specially designed for our Colonial Line of matched appliances. Chromium plated, its bright gleaming surface and permanent beauty gives added sales appeal when made a part of these sets. It will not discolor and is easy to clean. Makes an excellent cocktail server when used alone. Faced with protecting tissue, carefully wrapped and packed into individual containers. Weight 3 lbs.

LUSTROUS CHROMIUM TRAYS *by Porcelier*

· 24 ·

Lighting Fixtures by Porcelier, catalog no. 54, 1943. Courtesy of Jenny Perotti.

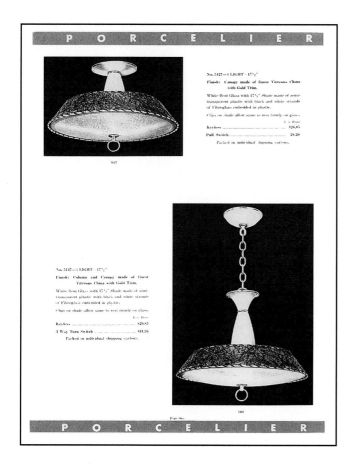

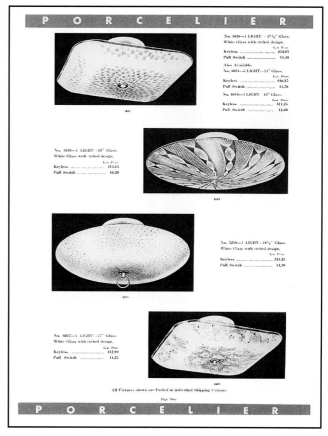

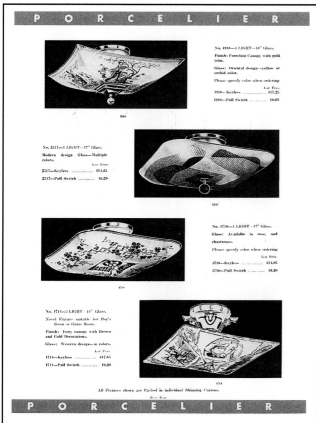

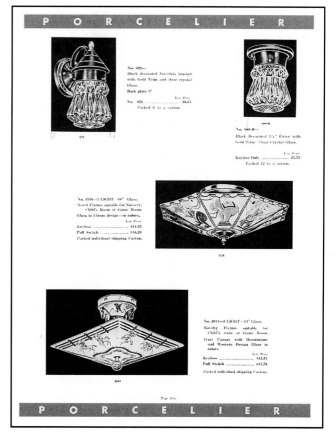

REPRINTS

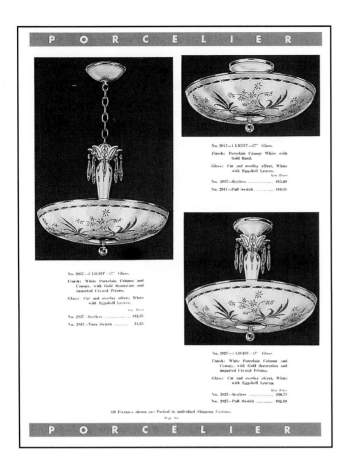

No. 2917—4 LIGHT—17" Glass.
Finish: Porcelain Canopy White with Gold Band.
Glass: Cut and overlay effect, White with Eggshell Leaves.

	List Price
No. 2917—Keyless	$15.60
No. 2917—Pull Switch	$16.95

No. 2907—4 LIGHT—17" Glass.
Finish: White Porcelain Column and Canopy, with Gold decoration and imported Crystal Prisms.
Glass: Cut and overlay effect, White with Eggshell Leaves.

	List Price
No. 2907—Keyless	$32.25
No. 2907—Turn Switch	$33.35

No. 2927—4 LIGHT—17" Glass.
Finish: White Porcelain Column and Canopy, with Gold decoration and imported Crystal Prisms.
Glass: Cut and overlay effect, White with Eggshell Leaves.

	List Price
No. 2927—Keyless	$30.75
No. 2927—Pull Switch	$32.10

All Fixtures shown are Packed in individual Shipping Cartons.

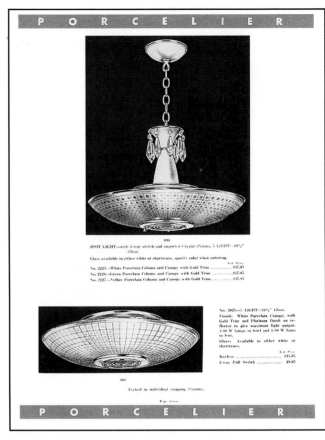

SPOT LIGHT—with 3-way switch and imported Crystal Prisms, 5 LIGHT—19½" Glass.
Glass available in either white or chartreuse, specify color when ordering.

	List Price
No. 2225—White Porcelain Column and Canopy with Gold Trim	$17.85
No. 2226—Green Porcelain Column and Canopy with Gold Trim	$17.85
No. 2227—Yellow Porcelain Column and Canopy with Gold Trim	$17.85

No. 2025—5 LIGHT—19½" Glass.
Finish: White Porcelain Canopy, with Gold Trim and Platinum finish on reflector to give maximum light output.

	List Price
Keyless	$25.85
3-way Pull Switch	$28.95

Packed in individual Shipping Cartons.

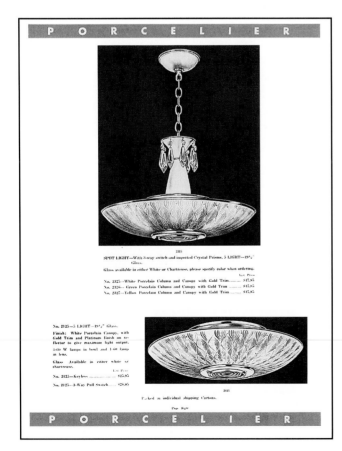

SPOT LIGHT—With 3-way switch and imported Crystal Prisms, 5 LIGHT—19½" Glass.
Glass available in either White or Chartreuse, please specify color when ordering.

	List Price
No. 2325—White Porcelain Column and Canopy with Gold Trim	$17.85
No. 2326—Green Porcelain Column and Canopy with Gold Trim	$17.85
No. 2327—Yellow Porcelain Column and Canopy with Gold Trim	$17.85

No. 2125—5 LIGHT—19½" Glass.
Finish: White Porcelain Canopy, with Gold Trim and Platinum finish on reflector to give maximum light output.

	List Price
No. 2125—Keyless	$25.85
No. 2125—3-Way Pull Switch	$28.95

Packed in individual shipping Cartons.

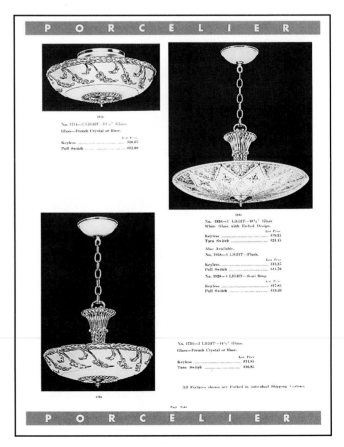

No. 1711—3 LIGHT—14½" Glass.
Glass—French Crystal or Rose.

	List Price
Keyless	$10.65
Pull Switch	$12.00

No. 1938—4 LIGHT—18½" Glass.
White Glass with Etched Design.

	List Price
Keyless	$19.35
Turn Switch	$21.15

Also Available.
No. 1918—1 LIGHT—Flush.

	List Price
Keyless	$13.35
Pull Switch	$14.70

No. 1926—1 LIGHT—Semi-Drop.

	List Price
Keyless	$17.85
Pull Switch	$19.20

No. 1731—3 LIGHT—14½" Glass.
Glass—French Crystal or Rose.

	List Price
Keyless	$11.85
Turn Switch	$16.95

All Fixtures shown are Packed in individual Shipping Cartons.

168

P O R C E L I E R

No. 9116—4 LIGHT—16" Glass.
Finish: Canopy made of finest Vitreous China decaled with flowers and 22 carat high lustre Gold Trim.

Lot Price
No. 9116—Keyless $17.25
No. 9116—Pull Switch $18.60

No. 9216—3 LIGHT—16" Glass.
Finish: Column and Canopy are made of finest Vitreous China Decaled with Flowers and 22 carat high lustre Gold Trim.

Lot Price
No. 9216—Keyless $25.35
No. 9216—Pull Switch $26.70

No. 9316—4 LIGHT—16" Glass.
Finish: Column and Canopy are made of finest Vitreous China decaled with flowers and 22 carat Gold Trim.

Lot Price
No. 9316—Keyless $26.85
No. 9316—Turn Switch $28.95

Glassware Made of fine fire-polished, pressed French Crystal Glass.
All Fixtures shown are Packed in individual Shipping Cartons.

P O R C E L I E R

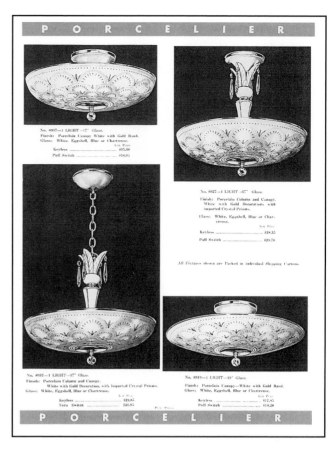

P O R C E L I E R

No. 8917—4 LIGHT—17" Glass.
Finish: Porcelain Canopy White with Gold Band.
Glass: White, Eggshell, Blue or Chartreuse.

Lot Price
Keyless $15.60
Pull Switch $16.95

No. 8927—4 LIGHT—17" Glass.
Finish: Porcelain Column and Canopy, White with Gold Decorations with imported Crystal Prisms.
Glass: White, Eggshell, Blue or Chartreuse.

Lot Price
Keyless $28.35
Pull Switch $29.70

All Fixtures shown are Packed in individual Shipping Cartons.

No. 8937—4 LIGHT—17" Glass.
Finish: Porcelain Column and Canopy, White with Gold Decorations, with imported Crystal Prisms.
Glass: White, Eggshell, Blue or Chartreuse.

Lot Price
Keyless $29.85
Turn Switch $31.95

No. 8919—4 LIGHT—19" Glass.
Finish: Porcelain Canopy—White with Gold Band.
Glass: White, Eggshell, Blue or Chartreuse.

Lot Price
Keyless $17.85
Pull Switch $19.20

P O R C E L I E R

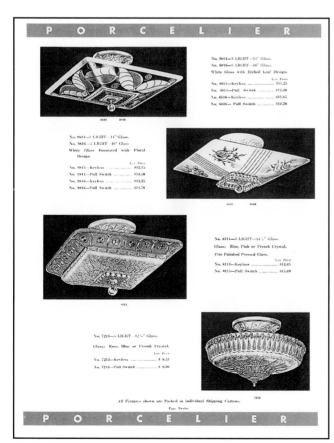

P O R C E L I E R

No. 6811—3 LIGHT—14" Glass.
No. 6816—5 LIGHT—16" Glass.
White Glass with Etched Leaf Design.

Lot Price
No. 6811—Keyless $11.25
No. 6811—Pull Switch $12.60
No. 6816—Keyless $11.85
No. 6816—Pull Switch $13.20

No. 9811—4 LIGHT—14" Glass.
No. 9816—4 LIGHT—16" Glass.
White Glass Decorated with Floral Design

Lot Price
No. 9811—Keyless $12.15
No. 9811—Pull Switch $13.50
No. 9816—Keyless $13.35
No. 9816—Pull Switch $14.70

No. 8111—3 LIGHT—14½" Glass.
Glass: Blue, Pink or French Crystal.
Fire Polished Pressed Glass.

Lot Price
No. 8111—Keyless $13.65
No. 8111—Pull Switch $15.00

No. 7213—3 LIGHT—12½" Glass.
Glass: Rose, Blue or French Crystal.

Lot Price
No. 7213—Keyless .... $ 8.55
No. 7213—Pull Switch .... $ 9.90

All Fixtures shown are Packed in individual Shipping Cartons.

Page Twelve

P O R C E L I E R

P O R C E L I E R

No. 4212—2 LIGHT—12½" Glass.
Glass: Rose, Blue or French Crystal.

Lot Price
No. 4212—Keyless .... $ 7.05
No. 4212—Pull Switch .... $ 8.40
Packed in individual shipping cartons.

No. 7212—2 LIGHT—12½" Glass.
Glass: Rose, Blue or French Crystal.

Lot Price
No. 7212—Keyless $7.95
No. 7212—Pull Switch $9.30
Packed in individual shipping cartons.

No. 1610—1 LIGHT—10½" Glass.
Glass: Rose, Blue or French Crystal.

Lot Price
No. 1610—Keyless .... $ 4.35
No. 1610—Pull Chain .... $ 4.95
Packed 6 to the shipping Carton.

No. 9110—1 LIGHT—10½" Glass.
Glass: Rose, Blue or French Crystal.

Lot Price
No. 9110—Keyless .... $ 4.05
No. 9110—Pull Chain .... $ 4.65
Packed 6 to the shipping Carton.

No. 1710—2 LIGHT—10½" Glass.
Glass: Rose, Blue or French Crystal.

Lot Price
No. 1710—Keyless .... $ 5.70
No. 1710—Pull Switch .... $ 7.05
Packed 6 to the shipping Carton.

Page Thirteen

P O R C E L I E R

P O R C E L I E R

Attractive Two-Light Brackets
Will Take Two-100 Watt Lamps

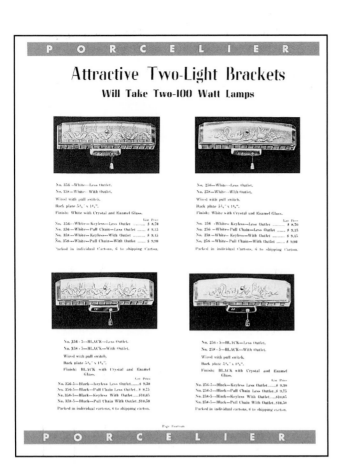

No. 358—White—Less Outlet.
No. 358—White—With Outlet.
Wired with pull switch.
Back plate 5½″ x 1½″.
Finish: White with Crystal and Enamel Glass.

No. 256—White—Less Outlet.
No. 258—White—With Outlet.
Wired with pull switch.
Back plate 5½″ x 1½″.
Finish: White with Crystal and Enamel Glass.

	List Price
No. 356—White—Keyless—Less Outlet	$ 8.70
No. 356—White—Pull Chain—Less Outlet	$ 9.15
No. 358—White—Keyless—With Outlet	$ 9.15
No. 358—White—Pull Chain—With Outlet	$ 9.90

Packed in individual Cartons, 6 to shipping Carton.

	List Price
No. 256—White—Keyless—Less Outlet	$ 8.70
No. 256—White—Pull Chain—Less Outlet	$ 9.15
No. 258—White—Keyless—With Outlet	$ 9.15
No. 258—White—Pull Chain—With Outlet	$ 9.90

Packed in individual Cartons, 6 to shipping Carton.

No. 356-5—BLACK—Less Outlet.
No. 358-5—BLACK—With Outlet.
Wired with pull switch.
Back plate 5½″ x 1½″.
Finish: BLACK with Crystal and Enamel Glass.

No. 256-5—BLACK—Less Outlet.
No. 258-5—BLACK—With Outlet.
Wired with pull switch.
Back plate 5½″ x 1½″.
Finish: BLACK with Crystal and Enamel Glass.

	List Price
No. 356-5—Black—Keyless Less Outlet	$ 9.30
No. 356-5—Black—Pull Chain Less Outlet	$ 9.75
No. 358-5—Black—Keyless With Outlet	$10.05
No. 358-5—Black—Pull Chain With Outlet	$10.50

Packed in individual cartons, 6 to shipping carton.

	List Price
No. 256-5—Black—Keyless Less Outlet	$ 9.30
No. 256-5—Black—Pull Chain Less Outlet	$ 9.75
No. 258-5—Black—Keyless With Outlet	$10.05
No. 258-5—Black—Pull Chain With Outlet	$10.50

Packed in individual cartons, 6 to shipping carton.

Page Fourteen

P O R C E L I E R

P O R C E L I E R

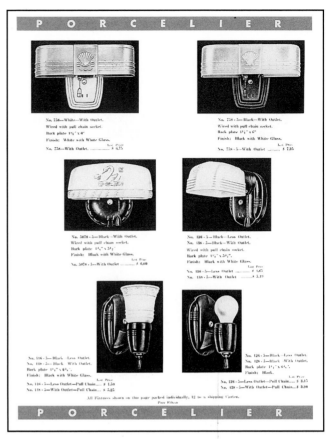

No. 758—White—With Outlet.
Wired with pull chain socket.
Back plate 1½″ x 6″.
Finish: White with White Glass.

	List Price
No. 758—With Outlet	$ 6.75

No. 758-5—Black—With Outlet.
Wired with pull chain socket.
Back plate 1½″ x 6″.
Finish: Black with White Glass.

	List Price
No. 758-5—With Outlet	$ 7.35

No. 5078-5—Black—With Outlet.
Wired with pull chain socket.
Back plate 1¾″ x 5½″.
Finish: Black with White Glass.

	List Price
No. 5078-5—With Outlet	$ 6.60

No. 136-5—Black—Less Outlet.
No. 138-5—Black—With Outlet.
Wired with pull chain socket.
Back plate 1¾″ x 5½″.
Finish: Black with White Glass.

	List Price
No. 136-5—Less Outlet	$ 4.65
No. 138-5—With Outlet	$ 5.10

No. 116-5—Black—Less Outlet.
No. 118-5—Black—With Outlet.
Back plate 1¾″ x 6½″.
Finish: Black with White Glass.

	List Price
No. 116-5—Less Outlet—Pull Chain	$ 4.50
No. 118-5—With Outlet—Pull Chain	$ 5.25

No. 126-5—Black—Less Outlet.
No. 128-5—Black—With Outlet.
Back plate 1¾″ x 6½″.
Finish: Black.

	List Price
No. 126-5—Less Outlet—Pull Chain	$ 3.15
No. 128-5—With Outlet—Pull Chain	$ 3.90

All Fixtures shown on this page packed individually, 12 to a shipping Carton.

Page Fifteen

P O R C E L I E R

P O R C E L I E R

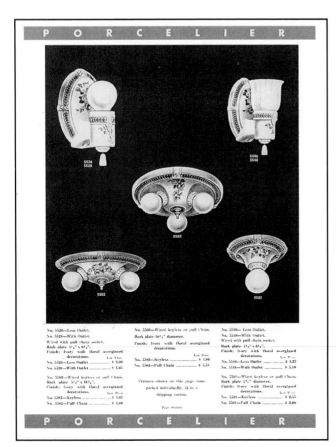

5526
5528

5546
5548

5503

5502

5501

No. 5526—Less Outlet.
No. 5528—With Outlet.
Wired with pull chain socket.
Back plate 1½″ x 6½″.
Finish: Ivory with floral overglazed decorations.

	List Price
No. 5526—Less Outlet	$ 3.30
No. 5528—With Outlet	$ 3.65

No. 5502—Wired keyless or pull chain.
Back plate 5½″ x 10½″.
Finish: Ivory with floral overglazed decorations.

	List Price
No. 5502—Keyless	$ 1.65
No. 5502—Pull Chain	$ 1.80

No. 5503—Wired keyless or pull chain.
Back plate 10½″ diameter.
Finish: Ivory with floral overglazed decorations.

	List Price
No. 5503—Keyless	$ 1.80
No. 5503—Pull Chain	$ 1.55

No. 5546—Less Outlet.
No. 5548—With Outlet.
Wired with pull chain socket.
Back plate 1½″ x 6½″.
Finish: Ivory with floral overglazed decorations.

	List Price
No. 5546—Less Outlet	$ 1.35
No. 5548—With Outlet	$ 5.10

No. 5501—Wired keyless or pull chain.
Back plate 5½″ diameter.
Finish: Ivory with floral overglazed decorations.

	List Price
No. 5501—Keyless	$ 2.55
No. 5501—Pull Chain	$ 3.00

Fixtures shown on this page come packed individually, 12 to a shipping carton.

Page Sixteen

P O R C E L I E R

P O R C E L I E R

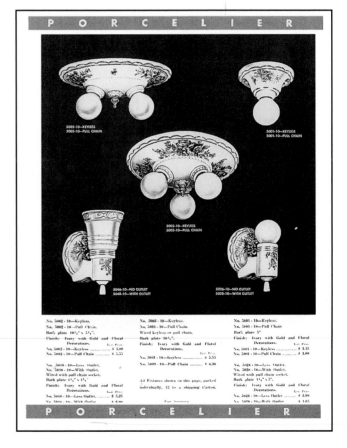

5002-10—KEYLESS
5002-10—PULL CHAIN

5001-10—KEYLESS
5001-10—PULL CHAIN

5003-10—KEYLESS
5003-10—PULL CHAIN

5046-10—NO OUTLET
5048-10—WITH OUTLET

5026-10—NO OUTLET
5028-10—WITH OUTLET

No. 5002-10—Keyless.
No. 5002-10—Pull Chain.
Wired keyless or pull chain.
Back plate 10½″.
Finish: Ivory with Gold and Floral Decorations.

	List Price
No. 5002-10—Keyless	$ 1.80
No. 5002-10—Pull Chain	$ 1.55

No. 5016-10—Less Outlet.
No. 5018-10—With Outlet.
Wired with pull chain socket.
Back plate 1½″ x 1½″.
Finish: Ivory with Gold and Floral Decorations.

	List Price
No. 5016-10—Less Outlet	$ 5.25
No. 5018-10—With Outlet	$ 6.00

No. 5003-10—Keyless.
No. 5003-10—Pull Chain.
Wired keyless or pull chain.
Back plate 10½″.
Finish: Ivory with Gold and Floral Decorations.

	List Price
No. 5003-10—Keyless	$ 1.80
No. 5003-10—Pull Chain	$ 6.30

No. 5001-10—Keyless.
No. 5001-10—Pull Chain.
Back plate 5″.
Finish: Ivory with Gold and Floral Decorations.

	List Price
No. 5001-10—Keyless	$ 3.15
No. 5001-10—Pull Chain	$ 3.60

No. 5026-10—Less Outlet.
No. 5028-10—With Outlet.
Wired with pull chain socket.
Back plate 1¾″ x 5″.
Finish: Ivory with Gold and Floral Decorations.

	List Price
No. 5026-10—Less Outlet	$ 3.90
No. 5028-10—With Outlet	$ 4.65

All Fixtures shown on this page, packed individually, 12 to a shipping Carton.

Page Seventeen

P O R C E L I E R

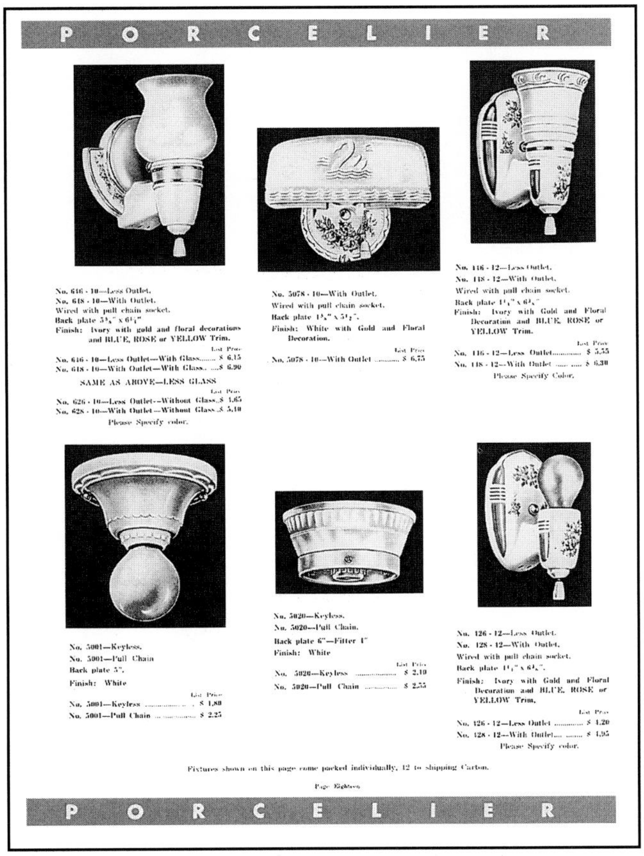

P O R C E L I E R

No. 616 - 10—Less Outlet.
No. 618 - 10—With Outlet.
Wired with pull chain socket.
Back plate $5\frac{3}{8}$" x $6\frac{1}{4}$"
Finish: Ivory with gold and floral decorations and BLUE, ROSE or YELLOW Trim.

List Price
No. 616 - 10—Less Outlet—With Glass........ $ 6.15
No. 618 - 10—With Outlet—With Glass.. ....$ 6.90

SAME AS ABOVE—LESS GLASS

List Price
No. 626 - 10—Less Outlet—Without Glass..$ 4.65
No. 628 - 10—With Outlet—Without Glass..$ 5.40

Please Specify color.

No. 5078 - 10—With Outlet.
Wired with pull chain socket.
Back plate $1\frac{3}{8}$" x $5\frac{1}{2}$".
Finish: White with Gold and Floral Decoration.

List Price
No. 5078 - 10—With Outlet .... $ 6.75

No. 116 - 12—Less Outlet.
No. 118 - 12—With Outlet.
Wired with pull chain socket.
Back plate $1\frac{1}{4}$" x $6\frac{3}{8}$"
Finish: Ivory with Gold and Floral Decoration and BLUE, ROSE or YELLOW Trim.

List Price
No. 116 - 12—Less Outlet............ $ 5.55
No. 118 - 12—With Outlet .... $ 6.30

Please Specify Color.

No. 5001—Keyless.
No. 5001—Pull Chain
Back plate 5".
Finish: White

List Price
No. 5001—Keyless .... $ 1.80
No. 5001—Pull Chain .... $ 2.25

No. 5020—Keyless.
No. 5020—Pull Chain.
Back plate 6"—Fitter 4"
Finish: White

List Price
No. 5020—Keyless .... $ 2.10
No. 5020—Pull Chain .... $ 2.55

No. 126 - 12—Less Outlet.
No. 128 - 12—With Outlet.
Wired with pull chain socket.
Back plate $1\frac{1}{4}$" x $6\frac{3}{8}$".
Finish: Ivory with Gold and Floral Decoration and BLUE, ROSE or YELLOW Trim.

List Price
No. 126 - 12—Less Outlet .... $ 4.20
No. 128 - 12—With Outlet.... .... $ 4.95

Please Specify color.

Fixtures shown on this page come packed individually, 12 to shipping Carton.

Page Eighteen

P O R C E L I E R

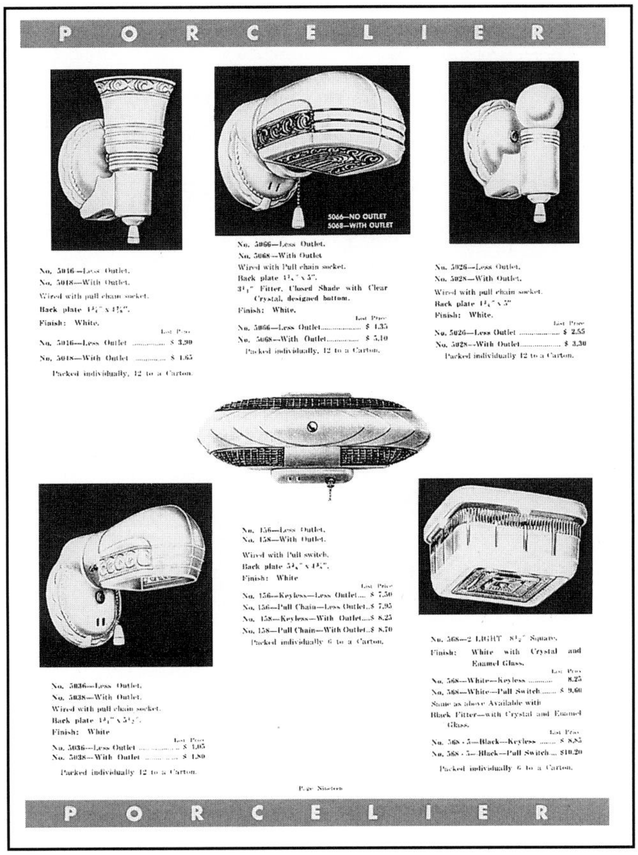

P O R C E L I E R

No. 5016—Less Outlet.
No. 5018—With Outlet.
Wired with pull chain socket.
Back plate $1\frac{3}{4}$" x $4\frac{7}{8}$".
Finish: White.

List Price
No. 5016—Less Outlet .... $ 3.90
No. 5018—With Outlet .... $ 4.65

Packed individually, 12 to a Carton.

5066—NO OUTLET
5068—WITH OUTLET

No. 5066—Less Outlet.
No. 5068—With Outlet
Wired with Pull chain socket.
Back plate $1\frac{3}{8}$" x 5".
$3\frac{1}{4}$" Fitter, Closed Shade with Clear Crystal, designed bottom.
Finish: White.

List Price
No. 5066—Less Outlet.................. $ 4.35
No. 5068—With Outlet.............. $ 5.10

Packed individually, 12 to a Carton.

No. 5026—Less Outlet.
No. 5028—With Outlet.
Wired with pull chain socket.
Back plate $1\frac{3}{4}$" x 5"
Finish: White.

List Price
No. 5026—Less Outlet .... $ 2.55
No. 5028—With Outlet.................. $ 3.30

Packed individually 12 to a Carton.

No. 156—Less Outlet.
No. 158—With Outlet.
Wired with Pull switch.
Back plate $5\frac{3}{8}$" x $4\frac{5}{8}$".
Finish: White

List Price
No. 156—Keyless—Less Outlet.... $ 7.50
No. 156—Pull Chain—Less Outlet..$ 7.95
No. 158—Keyless—With Outlet....$ 8.25
No. 158—Pull Chain—With Outlet..$ 8.70

Packed individually 6 to a Carton.

No. 5036—Less Outlet.
No. 5038—With Outlet.
Wired with pull chain socket.
Back plate $1\frac{3}{4}$" x $5\frac{1}{2}$".
Finish: White

List Price
No. 5036—Less Outlet .... $ 4.05
No. 5038—With Outlet .... $ 4.80

Packed individually 12 to a Carton.

No. 568—2 LIGHT $8\frac{1}{2}$" Square.
Finish: White with Crystal and Enamel Glass.

List Price
No. 568—White—Keyless 8.25
No. 568—White—Pull Switch....... $ 9.60

Same as above Available with Black Fitter—with Crystal and Enamel Glass.

List Price
No. 568 - 5—Black—Keyless .... $ 8.85
No. 568 - 5—Black—Pull Switch.... $10.20

Packed individually 6 to a Carton.

Page Nineteen

P O R C E L I E R

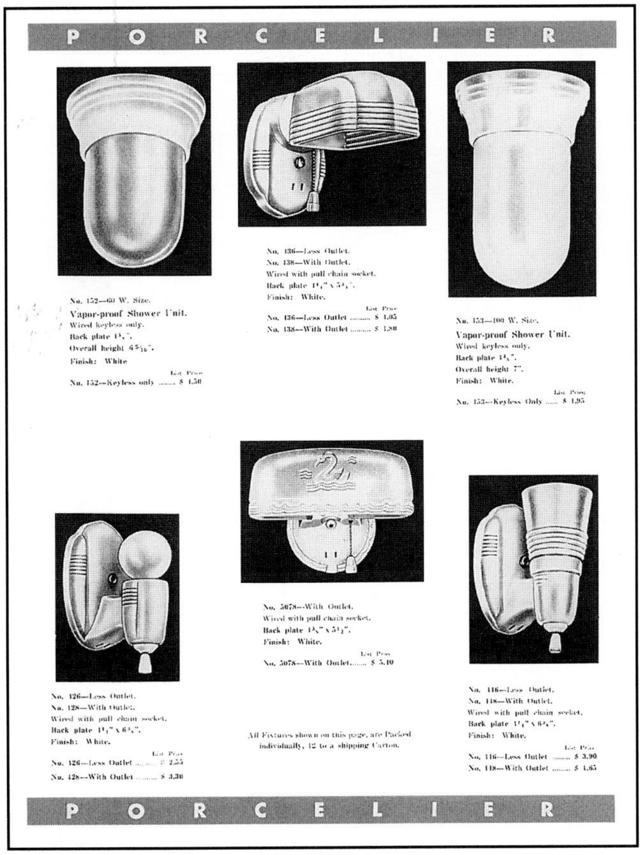

P O R C E L I E R

No. 152—60 W. Size.
Vapor-proof Shower Unit.
Wired keyless only.
Back plate $1\frac{3}{8}$".
Overall height $6\frac{5}{16}$".
Finish: White

List Price
No. 152—Keyless only .... $ 4.50

No. 136—Less Outlet.
No. 138—With Outlet.
Wired with pull chain socket.
Back plate $1\frac{1}{4}$" x $5\frac{3}{4}$".
Finish: White.

List Price
No. 136—Less Outlet .... $ 4.05
No. 138—With Outlet .... $ 4.80

No. 153—100 W. Size.
Vapor-proof Shower Unit.
Wired keyless only.
Back plate $1\frac{3}{8}$".
Overall height 7".
Finish: White.

List Price
No. 153—Keyless Only ...... $ 4.95

No. 126—Less Outlet.
No. 128—With Outlet.
Wired with pull chain socket.
Back plate $1\frac{1}{4}$" x $6\frac{3}{8}$".
Finish: White.

List Price
No. 126—Less Outlet .... $ 2.55
No. 128—With Outlet .... $ 3.30

No. 5078—With Outlet.
Wired with pull chain socket.
Back plate $1\frac{3}{8}$" x $5\frac{1}{2}$".
Finish: White.

List Price
No. 5078—With Outlet....... $ 5.10

All Fixtures shown on this page, are Packed individually, 12 to a shipping Carton.

No. 116—Less Outlet.
No. 118—With Outlet.
Wired with pull chain socket.
Back plate $1\frac{1}{4}$" x $6\frac{3}{8}$".
Finish: White.

List Price
No. 116—Less Outlet .... $ 3.90
No. 118—With Outlet .... $ 4.65

P O R C E L I E R

Lighting Fixtures by Porcelier, catalog no. 151, 1951.

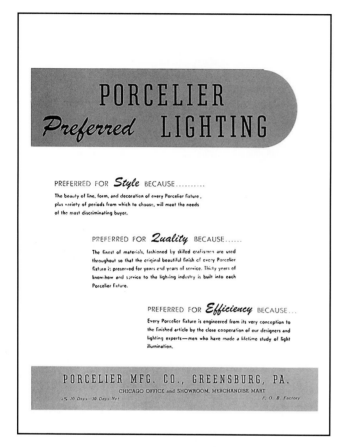

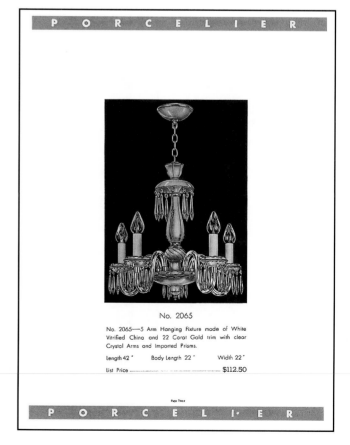

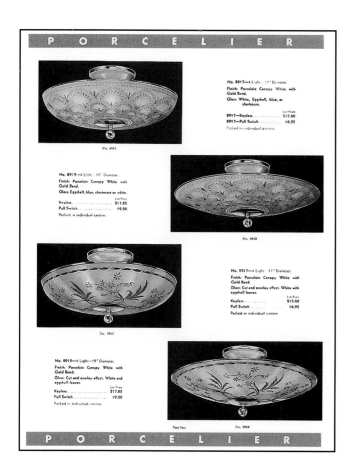

No. 8917—4 Light—17" Diameter.
Finish: Porcelain Canopy White with Gold Band.
Glass: White, Eggshell, blue, or chartreuse.

	List Price
8917—Keyless	$15.60
8917—Pull Switch	16.95

Packed in individual cartons.

No. 8919—4 Light—19" Diameter.
Finish: Porcelain Canopy White with Gold Band.
Glass: Eggshell, blue, chartreuse or white.

	List Price
Keyless	$17.85
Pull Switch	19.20

Packed in individual cartons.

No. 8917—4 Light—17" Diameter.
Finish: Porcelain Canopy White with Gold Band.
Glass: Cut and overlay effect. White with eggshell leaves.

	List Price
Keyless	$15.60
Pull Switch	16.95

Packed in individual cartons.

No. 8919—4 Light—19" Diameter.
Finish: Porcelain Canopy White with Gold Band.
Glass: Cut and overlay effect. White and eggshell leaves.

	List Price
Keyless	$17.85
Pull Switch	19.20

Packed in individual cartons.

No. 8917
No. 8919
No. 8917
No. 8919
Page Four

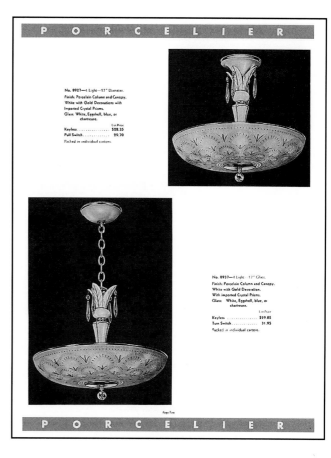

No. 8927—4 Light—17" Diameter.
Finish: Porcelain Column and Canopy. White with Gold Decorations with Imported Crystal Prisms.
Glass: White, Eggshell, blue, or chartreuse.

	List Price
Keyless	$28.35
Pull Switch	29.70

Packed in individual cartons.

No. 8937—4 Light—17" Glass.
Finish: Porcelain Column and Canopy. White with Gold Decoration. With imported Crystal Prisms.
Glass: White, Eggshell, blue, or chartreuse.

	List Price
Keyless	$19.85
Turn Switch	31.95

Packed in individual cartons.

Page Five

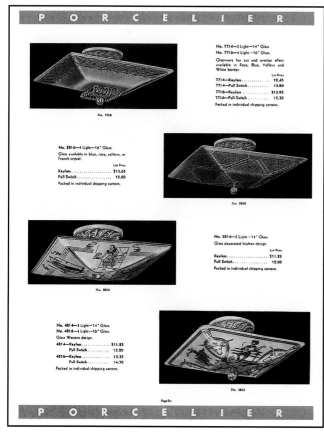

No. 7714—3 Light—14" Glass
No. 7716—4 Light—16" Glass.
Glassware has cut and overlay effect available in Rose, Blue, Yellow and White border.

	List Price
7714—Keyless	12.45
7714—Pull Switch	13.80
7716—Keyless	$13.95
7716—Pull Switch	15.30

Packed in individual shipping cartons.

No. 2816—4 Light—16" Glass.
Glass available in blue, rose, yellow, or French crystal.

	List Price
Keyless	$13.65
Pull Switch	15.00

Packed in individual shipping cartons.

No. 3814—3 Light—14" Glass.
Glass decorated kitchen design.

	List Price
Keyless	$11.25
Pull Switch	12.60

Packed in individual shipping cartons.

No. 4814—3 Light—14" Glass.
No. 4816—4 Light—16" Glass.
Glass Western design.

	List Price
4814—Keyless	$11.85
Pull Switch	13.20
4816—Keyless	13.35
Pull Switch	14.70

Packed in individual shipping cartons.

No. 7714
No. 2816
No. 3814
No. 4814
Page Six

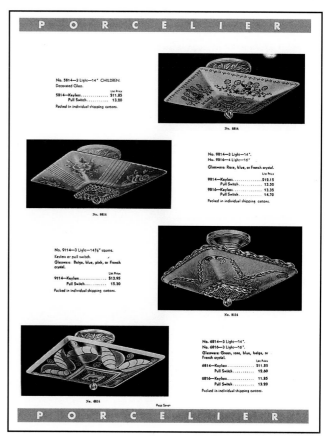

No. 5814—3 Light—14" CHILDREN.
Decorated Glass.

	List Price
5814—Keyless	$11.85
Pull Switch	13.20

Packed in individual shipping cartons.

No. 9814—3 Light—14".
No. 9816—4 Light—16".
Glassware: Rose, blue, or French crystal.

	List Price
9814—Keyless	$12.15
Pull Switch	13.50
9816—Keyless	13.35
Pull Switch	14.70

Packed in individual shipping cartons.

No. 9114—3 Light—14½" square.
Keyless or pull switch.
Glassware: Beige, blue, pink, or French crystal.

	List Price
9114—Keyless	$13.95
Pull Switch	15.30

Packed in individual shipping cartons.

No. 6814—3 Light—14".
No. 6816—3 Light—16".
Glassware: Green, rose, blue, beige, or French crystal.

	List Price
6814—Keyless	$11.85
Pull Switch	13.20
6816—Keyless	11.85
Pull Switch	13.20

Packed in individual shipping cartons.

No. 5814
No. 9814
No. 9114
No. 6814
Page Seven

No. 3114—3 Light—14⅜" Diameter.
Finish: Porcelain Canopy White with Gold Trim.
Glass: French crystal with clear border and bottom.
French crystal with amber border and bottom.

Keyless $11.85
Pull Switch 13.20
Packed in individual shipping cartons.

No. 3214—3 Light—14⅜" Diameter.
Finish: Porcelain Column and Canopy White with Gold Trim.
Glass: French crystal with clear border and bottom.
French crystal with amber border and bottom.

Keyless $17.85
Pull Switch 19.20
Packed in individual shipping cartons.

No. 3314—3 Light—14⅜" Diameter.
Finish: Porcelain Column and Canopy White with Gold Trim.
Glass: French crystal with clear border and bottom.
French crystal with amber border and bottom.

Keyless $19.35
Turn Switch 21.45
Packed in individual shipping cartons.

7114—3 LT.—14"
7214—3 LT.—14"
7314—3 LT.—14"

No. 7114—3 Light—14".
Glass—Rose, blue, beige and crystal.
Finish: Porcelain holder—ivory with gold trim.
Keyless $13.95
Pull Switch 15.30

No. 7214—3 Light—14".
Glass—Rose, blue, beige and crystal.
Finish: Canopy and column—porcelain with floral and gold decoration.
Keyless $19.95
Pull Switch 21.30

No. 7314—3 Light—14".
Glass—Rose, blue, beige and crystal.
Finish: Canopy and column—porcelain with floral and gold decoration.
Keyless $21.45
Turn Switch 23.55

All Fixtures Shown Are Shipped in Individual Cartons.

No. 8114—3 Light.
Keyless or pull switch.
Glass bowl diameter 14⅜".
Glass: Beige, blue, pink, or French crystal.
Fire Polished Pressed Glass.
No. 8114—Keyless $13.65
Pull Switch 15.00
Packed in individual shipping cartons.

No. 8314—3 Light—14⅜" Diameter.
Finish: Porcelain Column and Canopy with Floral and Gold Decoration.
Glass: Rose, blue, French crystal or beige.
Fire Polished Pressed Glass.
Keyless $19.95
Turn Switch 22.05
Packed in individual shipping cartons.

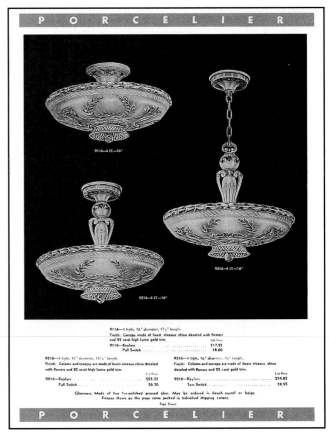

9116—4 LT.—16"
9216—4 LT.—16"
9316—4 LT.—16"

9116—4 light, 16" diameter, 7½" length
Finish: Canopy made of finest vitreous china decaled with flowers and 22 carat high lustre gold trim.
9116—Keyless $17.25
Pull Switch 18.60

9216—4 light, 16" diameter, 15½" length.
Finish: Column and canopy are made of finest vitreous china decaled with flowers and 22 carat high lustre gold trim.
9216—Keyless $25.35
Pull Switch 26.70

9316—4 light, 16" diameter, 16" length.
Finish: Column and canopy are made of finest vitreous china decaled with flowers and 22 carat gold trim.
9316—Keyless $26.85
Turn Switch 28.95

Glassware: Made of fine fire-polished pressed glass. May be ordered in french crystal or beige. Fixtures shown on this page come packed in individual shipping cartons.

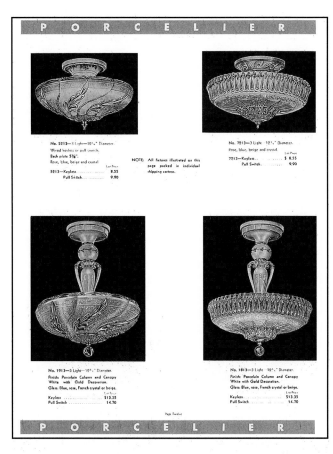

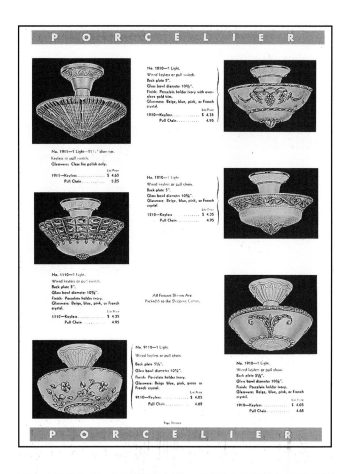

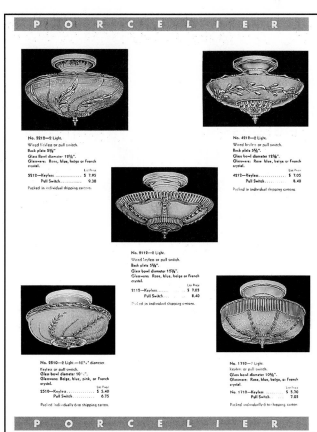

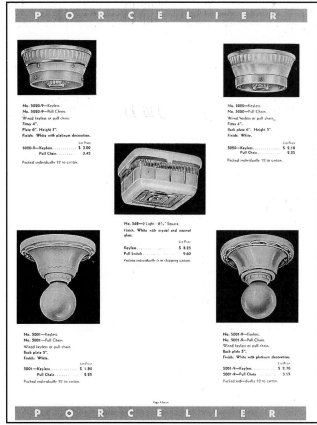

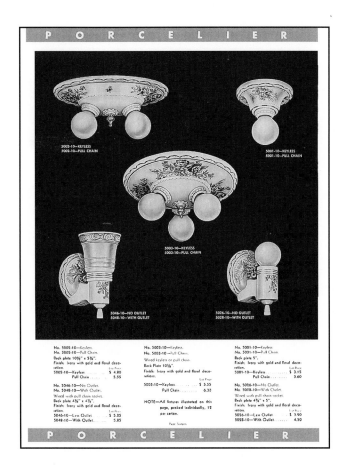

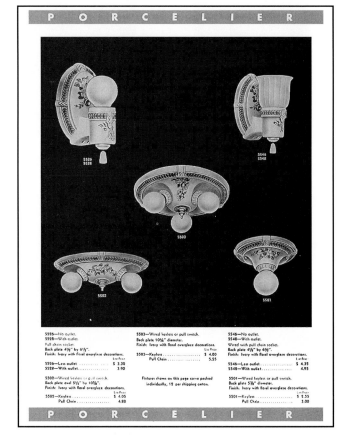

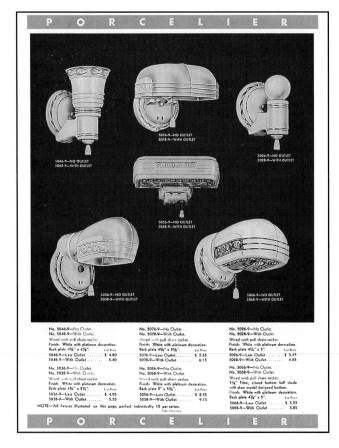

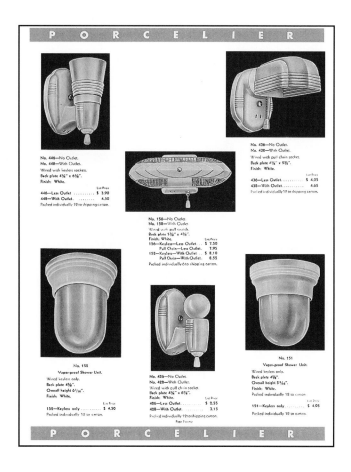

Store Catalog Reprints

Holsman Co. catalog reprint, 1938.

No. 20389. "Porcelier Percolator Set. Decorated China Percolator Service. The set consists of 8 cup Percolator with Sugar and Creamer to match. Comes in Old Ivory Finish with Beautiful Overglase Decoration and Platinum Striping. **$5.25** Per Set ....

No. 20293. Drip coffee maker. A beautiful 6 cup drip coffee maker of vitrified china. Decorative Old English Ivory with under glaze decoration. Top container of highly polished aluminum. Can be used as a tea pot.

Each **88c**

No. 20292. Three piece French Drip Coffee Set. Consisting of Drip Pot with Sugar and Creamer to match. Constructed of Vitrified china. Decorative Old English Ivory with under glaze decoration When the heavy gauged aluminum top has been removed can be used as teapot. Per set **$1.47**

No. 20291. Three piece Tea Set. Consisting of Tea Pot, Sugar and Creamer. Constructed of vitrified china. It is featured in decorative Old English Ivory with underglaze decoration.
Per Set **88c**

No. 20390. "Porceler" Urn Set. Extra Value China Urn Set. A remarkable low price for this 3 piece Coffee Service. Gracefully Decorated, Heat-Proof China. 9 cup Electric Urn. Floral Design.
Per Set **$5.40**

Montgomery Wards catalog reprints (various dates).

INEXPENSIVE UNSHADED FIXTURES—CHOICE OF THREE STYLES

Because of their direct light, which may result in eye strain, unshaded fixtures are not recommended for reading or working. For apartment halls, etc., however, they offer lowest cost fixtures possible. For better lighting, low prices, see shaded fixtures above.

GROUP D—Enameled Metal

Dainty Floral design embossed on Rich Ivory Enameled background. Body stamped from heavy steel. Our lowest priced fixtures.

(20) 583 B 8482—3-Light. 10½-in. diam. For wall switch. Ship. wt. 5 lbs..... **$1.25**

583 B 8463—3-Light with pull cord switch. Shipping weight, 5 lbs........... **$1.75**

(21) 83 B 8378—2-Light. Oval style. 12 by 6 in. For wall switch control. Shipping weight, 2 lbs.................... **72c**

83 B 8379—2-Light with pull cord.. **$1.05**

(22) 83 B 7558—1-Light Ceiling. 6⅜-in. diam. Plain socket. For wall switch control. Ship. wt. 1 lb. 8 oz........... **39c**

83 B 7559—1-Light with pull cord... **62c**

(23) 83 B 8382—1-Light Ceiling. 6⅜ in. diam. With socket ornament. For wall switch. Ship. wt. 1 lb. 6 oz......... **59c**

83 B 8385—1-Light with Pull cord.... **89c**

Use Ceramic coated bulbs on bulb page to reduce glare of unshaded fixtures. Eliminate filament glare—source of much eye strain—for they are coated on outside with smooth baked-on ceramic coating.

GROUP E—Glazed Porcelain

Rich Ivory finished baked on fixture. Colorful Basketweave pattern applied under glaze—won't wash off, can't fade. Guaranteed not to chip or peel. Dirt washes off with damp cloth. Bulbs not included.

(24) 583 B 8763—3-Light Ceiling. 10¼-in. diam. For wall switch. Wt. 4 lbs...... **$1.85**

583 B 8765—3-Light with pull cord.. **2.09**

(25) 83 B 8762—2-Light Ceiling. 6⅜ by 11 in. For wall switch control. Ship. wt. 3 lbs. 8 oz...................... **$1.35**

83 B 8764—2-Light with pull cord.. **1.59**

(26) 83 B 8761—1-Light. 5½-in. diam. With pull cord. Ship. wt. 1 lb. 12 oz..... **$1.00**

(27) 83 B 8760—1-Light Bracket. 6 by 4½-in. wall plate. Pull switch. Plug-in outlet always on. Ship. wt. 2 lbs......... **$1.25**

(28) Extra Wall Brackets. Cast metal. Two-tone Ivory enamel finish. On-off switch. Plug-in. Wall plate 4½ by 7½-in.

83 B 7555—With Ivory colored glass shade. Ship. wt. 2 lbs.................. **$2.00**

83 B 7554—Like above, but with candle instead of shade. Wt. 1 lb. 2 oz..... **$1.49**

GROUP F—Vitrified Chinaware

Colorful china fixtures with smooth Ivory finish. Decorated with floral rose design and highlighted with brilliant 14-karat Gold strippings. Edges of fixtures finished in either Blue or Dusty Coral to harmonize with floral design.

(29) 583 B 8778—2-Light Shaded. 10½-in. diam. Overall 8⅜ in. Blue or Coral glass shade with crystal glass louvers in bottom that throw light downward—diffuse it to protect eyes. For wall switch. Ship. wt. 3 lbs. 8 oz. **State Color.** Blue or Dusty Coral............ **$2.95**

(30) 583 B 8775—2-Light. 9¾ by 5½ in. For wall switch. Wt. 2 lbs. 2 oz. State Color: Blue or Dusty Coral..... **$1.55**

583 B 8776—2-Light with pull cord. State Color: Blue or Dusty Coral....... **$1.75**

(31) 583 B 8774—1-Light Ceiling. 7-in. diam. Pull chain switch. Ship. wt. 1 lb. 2 oz. State color. Blue or Dusty Coral... **$1.25**

(32) 583 B 8777—1-Light Bracket. 4 by 5½ in. wall plate. Turn switch. Wt. 1 lb. 6 oz. State Color: Blue or Coral.... **$1.45**

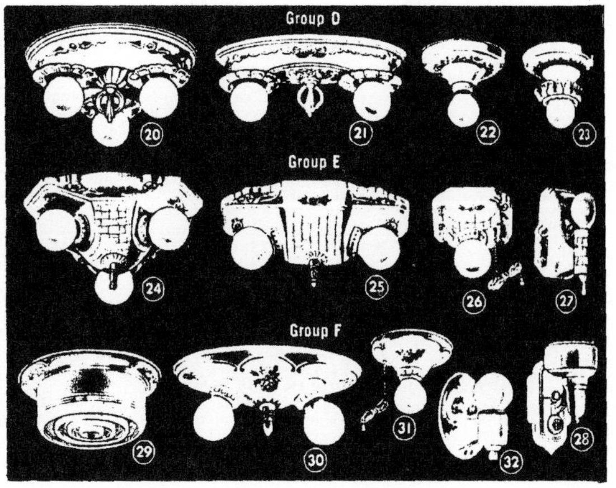

GROUP G—Cheery Porch Lights To Brighten Your Home, Welcome Your Guests

1942

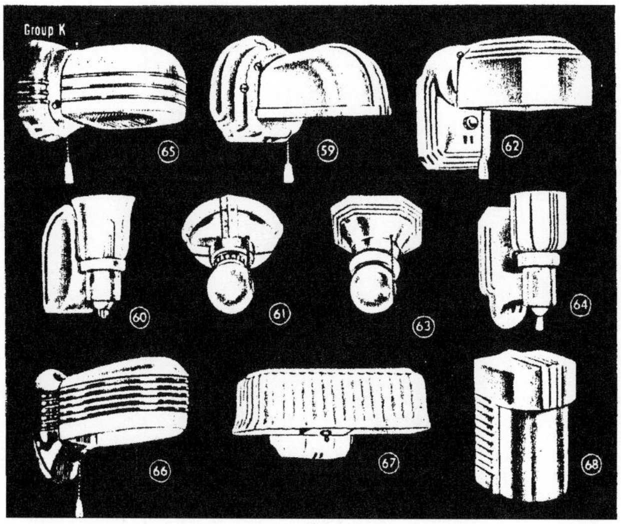

Ⓚ MATCHED GROUPS . . . PORCELAIN HOLDERS

Modern Beveled Procelain

Matched group of Porcelain with smooth flowing lines. Gleaming white surfaces—easy to keep clean. Cast—not pressed, for greater smoothness. All edges beveled, rounded, fit snugly against wall surface. Will take up to 60-watt bulbs.

(59) 83 B 8770—Shaded wall bracket. Use over sink, cabinet or stove. Snow-white glass shade with open bottom directs light where you need it. Plug-in outlet. Extends 8 in. Wall plate 4⅞ by 4⅞ in. Pull chain switch. Ship. wt. 2 lbs. 12 oz......... **$1.55**

(60) 83 B 8773—Shaded upright bracket. White Opal glass shade. Wall plate 4¼ by 5¾ in. Turn button switch controls light only; plug-in always on. Ship. wt. 2 lbs. 8 oz. **$1.49**

(61) 83 B 8769—1-Light Ceiling. Just right for small rooms or closets. 3-ft. pull cord. 5½-in. diam. holder. Ship wt. 1 lb. 12 oz................ **75c**

Octagonal Design

Sparkling White porcelain, with smart eight-sided design. Cast, (not pressed) for smoothness. Porcelain is shockproof, easy to clean. Take up to 60-watt bulbs. Bulbs not included.

(62) 83 B 8732—Shaded wall bracket. Open bottom. Snow white, blown glass shade. 4 by 5½-in. wall plate. Extends 7½ in. Plug-in outlet Pull chain switch Ship. wt. 3 lbs... **$1.45**

83 B 8730—Without plug-in... **1.35**

(63) 83 B 8733—Ceiling light. 5 in. diam. Pull cord switch with 3 ft. cord. White only. Wt. 2 lbs. 8 oz...... **72c**

(64) 83 B 8731—Shaded bracket. Snow white shade. 3⅝ by 6¾ in. holder. Extends 4 in. Pull chain switch. Plug-in. Ship. wt. 3 lbs. 8 oz... **$1.35**

83 B 8728—Like above but without shade. Ship. wt. 2 lbs. 4 oz.... **$1.10**

83 B 8746—Like above, but with no outlet...................... **92c**

Modern Shaded Brackets

(65) Enclosed White glass shade; crystal glass bottom. White porcelain holder. Plug-in outlet. Pull chain switch. 4½ in. high. 4¾ in. wide, extends 8 in. Takes up to 75-watt bulb.

83 B 8720—Wt. 2 lbs. 8 oz... **$1.95**

(66) 83 B 8188—Snow white glass shade with crystal lines. Chrome plated metal holder. 5⅛ in. high, 4⅛ in. wide, extends 7¼ in. Wt. 3 lbs. **$2.45**

(67) 2-Light Bracket for larger rooms. Satin finish White glass shade, 4½ by 10½-in. White porcelain holder 4½ by 5 in. Up to two 60-watt bulbs. On-off switch.

83 B 8771—Wt. 4 lbs. 8 oz... **$2.95**

(68) Use as shown or upside down. Snow-white glass shade with open bottom. Use up to 60-watt bulb. Plug-in. Push button. 6 by 3½ in. Extends 5 in. Ship. wt. 3 lbs.

83 B 8744—White porc. holder. **$1.95**

83 B 8745—Black porc. holder. **2.09**

1942

Colorful Vitreous China Coffee Makers

(A) All heatproof Vitreous China, drip-type Coffee Makers—no metal parts. China cover fits both sections. Use lower section of Coffee Maker with cover as teapot. Boiling water poured into heatproof Coffee Maker won't crack or craze it.

Your choice of two patterns. Nautical decoration in blue on Ivory color background. Gay or Dutch boy-and-girl and floral motif, vari-colored on Ivory color background. *Be sure to state pattern.*

Article No.	Cup Size	Ship. Wt.	Each
86 B 3402	2	2 lbs. 8 oz.	89c
586 B 3403	4	4 lbs.	$1.39
586 B 3404	6	4 lbs.	1.79
586 B 3405	8	6 lbs.	2.39

(B) **Three-Piece Coffee Maker Set** of finest heatproof Vitreous China. Set includes one 6-cup size drip-type Coffee Maker with matching Sugar and Creamer. Choice of two well designed patterns. Gay nautical decoration in Blue on Ivory color background, or boy-and-girl motif in 3 colors on Ivory background. *Be sure to state pattern.*

586 B 3401—3-Piece Set. Shipping weight 8 lbs. **$2.69**

1942

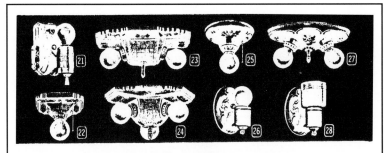

Vitrified Chinaware Fixtures

Inexpensive fixtures for use without shades. Rich Ivory finish is baked-on. Basketweave pattern applied before glaze—won't wash off, chip, peel or fade. Easy to clean. Not recommended for reading or working. Use Wards Eyesaver bulbs to eliminate glare . . . bulbs not included . . order from bulb page.

[21] 1-Light Bracket. 6 by 4½-in. wall plate. Plug-in outlet . . . always "on." 83 B 8760—On-off switch. Wt. 2 lbs. $1.25

[22] 1-Light Ceiling. 5½-in. diameter. 83 B 8761—Pull cord. Wt. 1 lb. 12 oz. $1.00

[23] 2-Lt. Ceiling. 6⅜ by 11 in. Wt. 3½ lbs. 83 B 8762L—For wall switch . . . . $1.35 83 B 8764L—Same but with pull cord 1.59

[24] 3-Lt. Ceiling. 10¼ in. Ship. wt. 4 lbs. 83 B 8763L—For wall switch . . . $1.85 83 B 8765L—Same but with pull cord 2.09

Colorful China fixtures. Smooth Ivory finish and embossed dainty floral design. 14 Karat Gold trim. Blue or dusty Coral edges. Use Wards Eyesaver bulbs to reduce glare . . . order from bulb page. For better lighting select fixtures above and on preceding pages. *When ordering, be sure to state color.*

[25] 1-Light Ceiling. 6 inches in diameter. With pull chain switch. 83 B 8774L—Ship. wt. 1 lb. 2 oz. $1.25

[26] 1-Light Bracket. Like (28) described below but without shade. 83 B 8777L—Ship. wt. 1 lb. 6 oz. . . . $1.45

[27] 2-Lt. Ceiling. 9¾x5½-in. Wt.2 lbs.2 oz. 83 B 8775L—For wall switch . . . $1.55 83 B 8776L—Same but with pull cord 1.75

[28] 1-Light Bracket. 4 by 5½-in. wall plate. Plug-in outlet for appliances . . current always "On." Ivory colored glass open-top shade. Ship. wt. 2 lbs. 83 B 8786L—On-off switch $2.19

978   WARDS   KS   Use Wards Time Payment Plan

1943/1944

National-Porges Corp. catalog reprint (1933).

ELECTRIC URN SETS AND PERCOLATORS

NEW PORCELIER ALL-CHINA ⟶ VITRIFIED HEAT-PROOF ELECTRIC PERCOLATOR SET

Beauty—of line, coloring, and workmanship. Made of heat-proof china.

Sanitary—absolute cleanliness and wholesomeness.

Versatile—all the qualities of a

No. 4N10 Porcelier Percolator Set Complete— With sugar and creamer Retail $9.50 Dealer's $5.25 Less 2% Cash

$5.14

thermos container, without harboring any unpleasantness of taste. Clean and sweet inside.

Coffee—that retains all of its purity, flavor, and aroma.

No. P4N10 Porcelier Percolator Only— 7 cup. Retail 7.50 Dealer's $4.15 Less 2% Cash

$4.07

180

Sears Roebuck catalog reprints (various dates).

Colorful China Smartly Designed

Bright birds wing their merry way in gay "Flight" design that decorates this handsome coffee maker. Made of vitrified heat-holding china in a warm lustrous ivory color. Gleaming, easy-to-clean aluminum inset. Capacity, 6 cups. Shipping weight, 4 lbs.

$1.49 3-pc. Set

11D3237—Coffee Maker only.......**98c**

11 D 1259—Complete 3-Pc. Set. consisting of Coffee Maker with matching Sugar and Creamer. Shpg. wt., 7 pounds...**$1.49**

1938

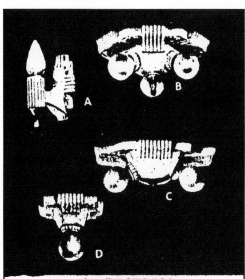

the FOSTORIA

Sears biggest value in porcelain fixtures. Toned ivory color porcelain. Attractive ribbed design decorated with colored floral motif.

$1.49 20 D 5196

Ⓑ 20 D 5196—3-Light. For wall switch. Length, 10 in. Width, 10 in. Shipping weight, 4 pounds.................**$1.49**

20 D 5197—Same as above, except with pull switch....**$1.79**

Ⓒ 20 D 5194—2-Light. For wall switch. 10¼x6¼ in. Shipping weight, 3 lbs......**94c**

20 D 5195—Same as above, except with pull switch....**$1.29**

Ⓐ 20 D 5198—1-Light Bracket. With on-off switch and appliance outlet. Length, 5¾ in. Width, 4 in. Shipping weight, 2 pounds.................**98c**

Ⓓ 20 D 5193—1-Light. With pull switch. Width, 5¾ in. Shipping wt., 2 lbs.........**79c**

1939/1940

Drip Coffee and Tea Maker

• 2-in-1 usefulness, as a 7-cup Drip coffee maker or a 9-cup teapot **$1.75**

• Makes the kind of coffee that wins friends

Makes really good coffee without metallic taste—brews refreshing tea. Won't crack or craze. Red and Black "Cattail" design on vitrified China base. No metal can touch coffee. Coffee basket is porcelain enameled steel. Lid fits both parts. Capacity: 7 cups as coffee-maker; 9 cups as teapot.

11 L 3238—Shpg. wt., 5 lbs.....**$1.75**

1942

U.S. Patent and Design Reprints

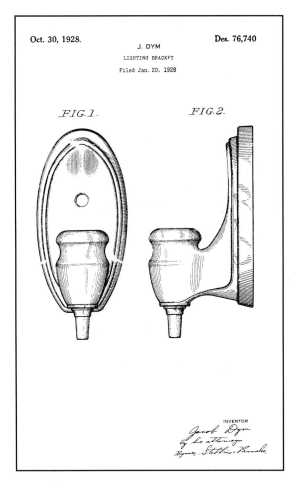

Oct. 30, 1928.

J. DYM

LIGHTING BRACKET

Filed Jan. 20, 1928

Des. 76,740

FIG. 1. *FIG. 2.*

INVENTOR

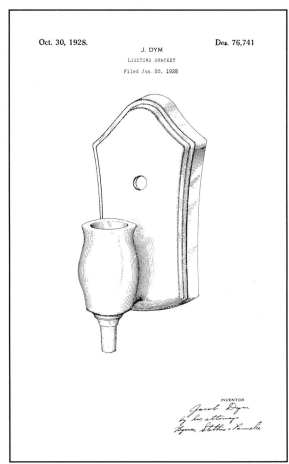

Oct. 30, 1928.

J. DYM

LIGHTING BRACKET

Filed Jan. 20, 1928

Des. 76,741

INVENTOR

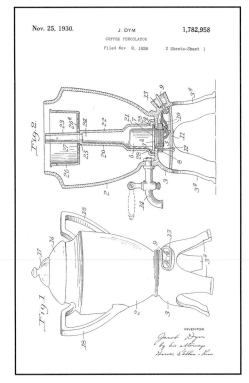

Nov. 25, 1930.

J. DYM

COFFEE PERCOLATOR

Filed Nov. 8, 1928

1,782,958

2 Sheets—Sheet 1

INVENTOR

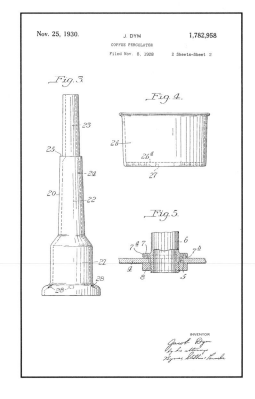

Nov. 25, 1930.

J. DYM

COFFEE PERCOLATOR

Filed Nov. 8, 1928

1,782,958

2 Sheets—Sheet 2

Fig. 3. *Fig. 4.* *Fig. 5.*

INVENTOR

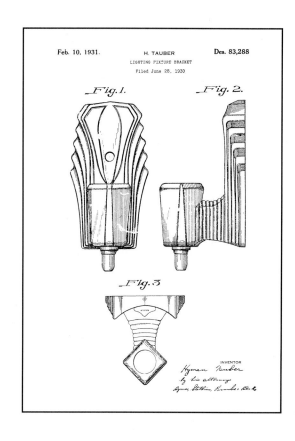

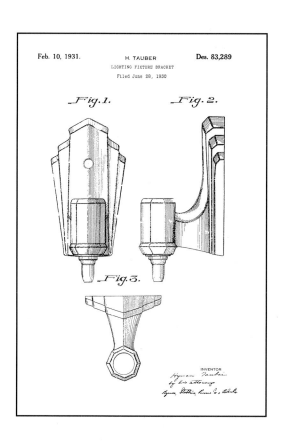

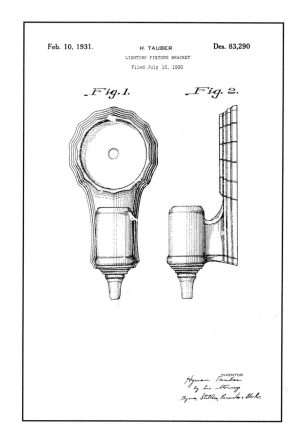

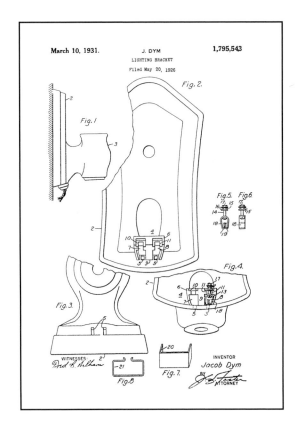

March 10, 1931. J. DYM 1,795,543
LIGHTING BRACKET
Filed May 20, 1926

Fig. 2.
Fig. 1.
Fig. 5. Fig. 6.
Fig. 3.
Fig. 4.
Fig. 7.
Fig. 8.

WITNESSES:
Fred C. Arthur

INVENTOR
Jacob Dym
BY
ATTORNEY

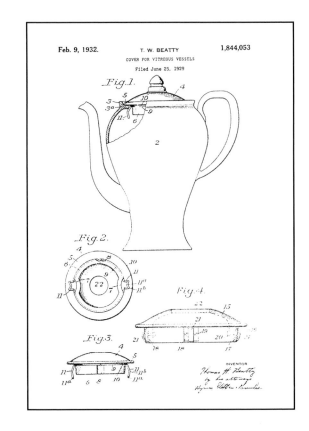

Feb. 9, 1932. T. W. BEATTY 1,844,053
COVER FOR VITREOUS VESSELS
Filed June 25, 1929

Fig. 1.
Fig. 2.
Fig. 3.
Fig. 4.

INVENTOR
Thomas W. Beatty
by his attorneys

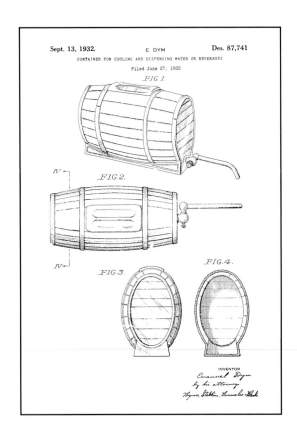

Sept. 13, 1932. E DYM Des. 87,741
CONTAINER FOR COOLING AND DISPENSING WATER OR BEVERAGES
Filed June 27, 1932

FIG. 1.
FIG. 2.
FIG. 3. FIG. 4.

INVENTOR
Emanuel Dym
by his attorneys

184

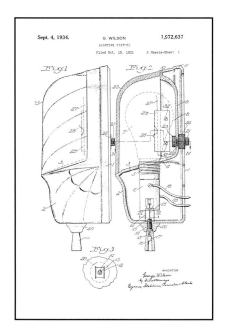

Sept. 4, 1934.   G. WILSON   1,972,637
LIGHTING FIXTURE
Filed Oct. 15, 1931   2 Sheets-Sheet 1

Fig.1   Fig.2

Fig.3

INVENTOR
George Wilson
by his attorneys
Byrnes Stebbins Parmelee & Blenk

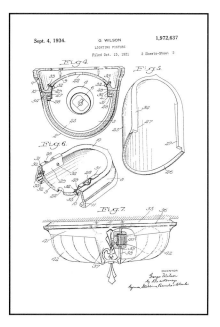

Sept. 4, 1934.   G. WILSON   1,972,637
LIGHTING FIXTURE
Filed Oct. 15, 1931   2 Sheets-Sheet 2

Fig.4   Fig.5

Fig.6

Fig.7

INVENTOR
George Wilson
by his attorneys
Byrnes Stebbins Parmelee & Blenk

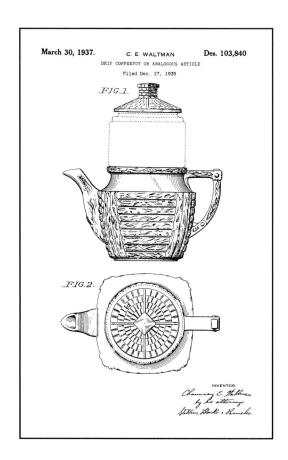

March 30, 1937.   C. E. WALTMAN   Des. 103,840
DRIP COFFEEPOT OR ANALOGOUS ARTICLE
Filed Dec. 17, 1935

FIG.1.

FIG.2.

INVENTOR
Chauncey E. Waltman
by his attorneys
Stebbins, Blenk & Parmelee

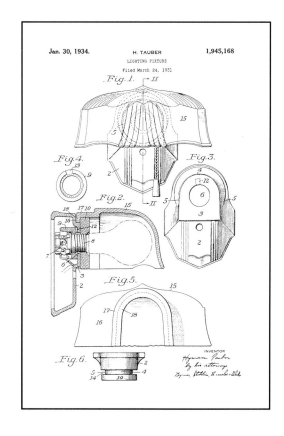

Jan. 30, 1934.   H. TAUBER   1,945,168
LIGHTING FIXTURE
Filed March 24, 1931

Fig.1.

Fig.4.   Fig.3.

Fig.2.

Fig.5.

Fig.6.

INVENTOR
Hyman Tauber
by his attorneys
Byrnes Stebbins Parmelee & Blenk

185

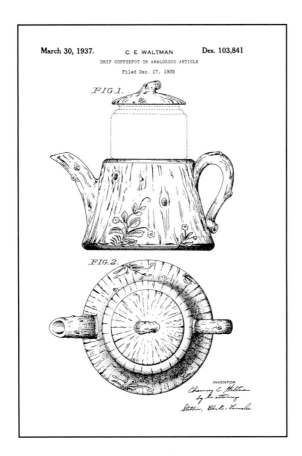

March 30, 1937.   C. E. WALTMAN   Des. 103,841

DRIP COFFEEPOT OR ANALOGOUS ARTICLE

Filed Dec. 17, 1935

FIG.1.

FIG.2.

INVENTOR

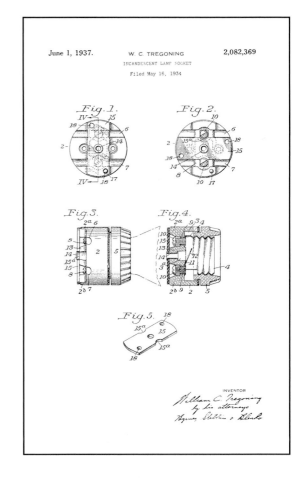

June 1, 1937.   W. C. TREGONING   2,082,369

INCANDESCENT LAMP SOCKET

Filed May 16, 1934

Fig.1.   Fig.2.

Fig.3.   Fig.4.

Fig.5.

INVENTOR

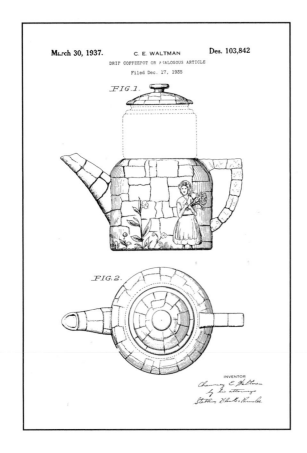

March 30, 1937.   C. E. WALTMAN   Des. 103,842

DRIP COFFEEPOT OR ANALOGOUS ARTICLE

Filed Dec. 17, 1935

FIG.1.

FIG.2.

INVENTOR

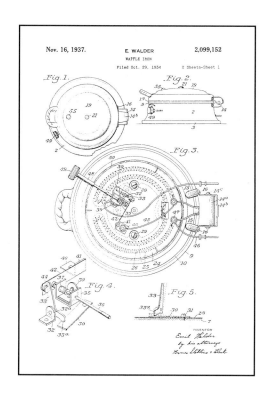

Nov. 16, 1937.   E. WALDER   2,099,152
WAFFLE IRON
Filed Oct. 29, 1934   2 Sheets-Sheet 1

Fig.1. Fig.2. Fig.3. Fig.4. Fig.5.

INVENTOR
Emil Walder
by his attorneys

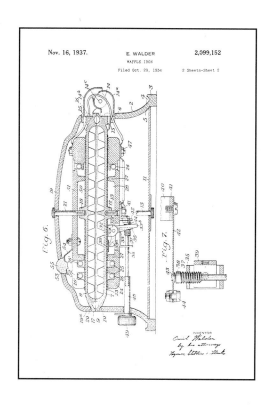

Nov. 16, 1937.   E. WALDER   2,099,152
WAFFLE IRON
Filed Oct. 29, 1934   2 Sheets-Sheet 2

Fig.6. Fig.7.

INVENTOR
Emil Walder
by his attorneys

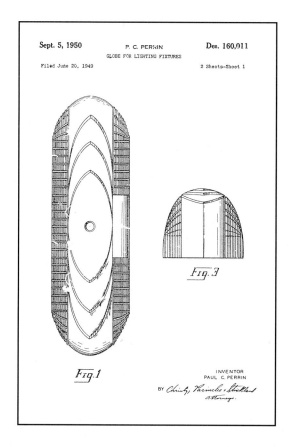

Sept. 5, 1950   P. C. PERRIN   Des. 160,011
GLOBE FOR LIGHTING FIXTURES
Filed June 20, 1949   2 Sheets-Sheet 1

Fig.1   Fig.3

INVENTOR
PAUL C. PERRIN
BY Christy, Parmelee, Strickland
attorneys.

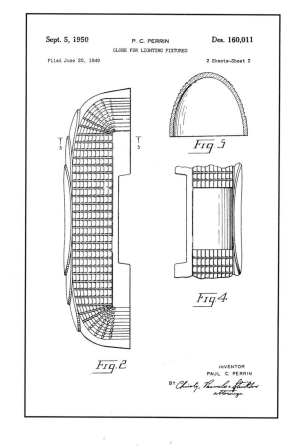

Sept. 5, 1950   P. C. PERRIN   Des. 160,011
GLOBE FOR LIGHTING FIXTURES
Filed June 20, 1949   2 Sheets-Sheet 2

Fig.2   Fig.4   Fig.5

INVENTOR
PAUL C. PERRIN
BY Christy, Parmelee, Strickland
attorneys.

187

Coffee maker instructions and company guarantee.

PORCELIER DRIP COFFEE MAKER
MAKES HEALTHFUL COFFEE

Now you can make full flavored Porcelier Drip Coffee day in and day out, without fuss or bother. The absence of boiling, eliminates the bitter taste; and retains the rich beneficial oils, and aroma.

Approved by the proving institutes; experts, and leading authorities.

Eliminates all guess work in the brewing of perfect coffee.

Makes uniformly delicious coffee at the approximate speed of one cup per minute.

Pin point perforations insure clear, sediment-free beverage.

The coffee maker extracts only the beneficial and stimulating oils from the coffee.

This is the method recommended by leading food and health authorities.

DIRECTIONS FOR BREWING PERFECT COFFEE

1. Place one rounded tablespoonful of "DRIP GRIND" coffee for each cup in the coffee basket. It is not advisable to have the coffee pulverized. Just "DRIP GRIND" coffee produces perfect results—DRIP GRIND is the universal term.

2. Cover coffee with small china "baffle plate." Pour in vigorously boiling water. Place the cover on top container and let stand until the water has all dripped through the coffee. Full bodied, rich, drip coffee becomes an automatic process with each meal.

3. For a neater appearance after coffee is made remove upper inset and serve your coffee at the table. The lid fits both sections.

NOTE: The fineness of the ground coffee controls the time necessary for the coffee making. Coffee which is too finely ground will require more time for making coffee than will a coarser grind. When buying coffee for this coffee maker, we suggest you ask for "DRIP GRIND" in your favorite brand of coffee.

DO NOT PLACE CHINA POT OVER OPEN FLAME—USE ASBESTOS OR METAL PAD

The manufacturer will not be responsible for any damage caused due to placing china pot over open flame.

Manufactured by **PORCELIER MANUFACTURING COMPANY** Greensburg, Pa.

Printed in U. S. A.

Guarantee

This percolator is guaranteed against mechanical and electrical defects for a period of one year from date of sale to user, provided that it is used in accordance with the following instructions:

1. When cleaning, don't immerse pot in water.
2. Make sure that there is some water in the percolator before plugging in.
3. Use this percolator with 115 Volts 450 Watts A. C. current only.

The manufacturer will repair or replace defective parts under this guarantee if returned to the dealer or manufacturer, transportation charges prepaid.

PORCELIER MANUFACTURING COMPANY
Greensburg, Pennsylvania.

Suggestions How To Use Your Percolator

Pour into the percolator as many cups of cold water as you desire coffee. In the coffee basket, place a level tablespoon of ground coffee for each cup desired, and replace the strainer. Make sure that the pump is properly seated on the base or element. Pour about one-half cup of cold water over the coffee in the basket.

Make sure that there is some liquid in the percolator while it is connected to the current.

In using any appliance, it is always best to start and turn off at the appliance, and never by the switch.

If coffee is "held over," remove coffee basket and pump. You can reheat the coffee without the basket and pump, simply by connecting to the current.

Endnotes

[1]Lehner, Lois. *Lehner's Encyclopedia of U.S. Marks on Pottery, Porcelain & Clay.* Paducah, KY: Collector Books, 1988.

[2]*City of Greensburg "A History."* Westmoreland County Historical Society; Copyright June 1949.

[3]PPG, Industries, Real Estate Division, Pittsburgh, PA.

[4]Information obtained from past employees of Porcelier.

[5]Brewer, Don. *The Depression Glass Daze.* January 1984.

COLLECTOR BOOKS
Informing Today's Collector

BOOKS ON COLLECTIBLES

This is only a partial listing of the books on antiques that are available from Collector Books. All books are well illustrated and contain current values. Most of the following books are available from your local bookseller, antique dealer, or public library. If you are unable to locate certain titles in your area, you may order by mail from COLLECTOR BOOKS, P.O. Box 3009, Paducah, KY 42002-3009. Customers with Visa or MasterCard may phone in orders from 7:00–4:00 CST, Monday–Friday, Toll Free 1-800-626-5420. Add $2.00 for postage for the first book ordered and $0.30 for each additional book. Include item number, title, and price when ordering. Allow 14 to 21 days for delivery.

DOLLS, FIGURES & TEDDY BEARS

2382	**Advertising Dolls**, Identification & Values, Robison & Sellers	$9.95
2079	**Barbie** Doll Fashions, Volume I, Eames	$24.95
3957	**Barbie** Exclusives, Rana	$18.95
4557	**Barbie**, The First 30 Years, Deutsch	$24.95
3310	**Black Dolls**, 1820–1991, Perkins	$17.95
3873	**Black Dolls**, Book II, Perkins	$17.95
3810	**Chatty Cathy** Dolls, Lewis	$15.95
2021	Collectible **Action Figures**, 2nd Ed., Manos	$14.95
1529	Collector's Encyclopedia of **Barbie** Dolls, DeWein	$19.95
4506	Collector's Guide to **Dolls in Uniform**, Bourgeois	$18.95
3727	Collector's Guide to **Ideal Dolls**, Izen	$18.95
3728	Collector's Guide to Miniature **Teddy Bears**, Powell	$17.95
3967	Collector's Guide to **Trolls**, Peterson	$19.95
4569	**Howdy Doody**, Collector's Reference and Trivia Guide, Koch	$16.95
1067	**Madame Alexander** Dolls, Smith	$19.95
3971	**Madame Alexander** Dolls Price Guide #20, Smith	$9.95
3733	**Modern Collector's** Dolls, Sixth Series, Smith	$24.95
3991	**Modern Collector's** Dolls, Seventh Series, Smith	$24.95
4571	**Liddle Kiddles**, Identification & Value Guide, Langford	$18.95
3972	Patricia Smith's **Doll Values**, Antique to Modern, 11th Edition	$12.95
3826	Story of **Barbie**, Westenhouser	$19.95
1513	**Teddy Bears & Steiff** Animals, Mandel	$9.95
1817	**Teddy Bears & Steiff** Animals, 2nd Series, Mandel	$19.95
2084	**Teddy Bears, Annalee's & Steiff** Animals, 3rd Series, Mandel	$19.95
1808	Wonder of **Barbie**, Manos	$9.95
1430	World of **Barbie** Dolls, Manos	$9.95

FURNITURE

1457	American **Oak** Furniture, McNerney	$9.95
3716	American **Oak** Furniture, Book II, McNerney	$12.95
1118	Antique **Oak** Furniture, Hill	$7.95
2132	Collector's Encyclopedia of **American** Furniture, Vol. I, Swedberg	$24.95
2271	Collector's Encyclopedia of **American** Furniture, Vol. II, Swedberg	$24.95
3720	Collector's Encyclopedia of **American** Furniture, Vol. III, Swedberg	$24.95
1437	Collector's Guide to **Country** Furniture, Raycraft	$9.95
3878	Collector's Guide to **Oak** Furniture, George	$12.95
1755	Furniture of the **Depression Era**, Swedberg	$19.95
3906	**Heywood-Wakefield** Modern Furniture, Rouland	$18.95
1965	**Pine** Furniture, Our American Heritage, McNerney	$14.95
1885	**Victorian** Furniture, Our American Heritage, McNerney	$9.95
3829	**Victorian** Furniture, Our American Heritage, Book II, McNerney	$9.95
3869	**Victorian** Furniture books, 2 volume set, McNerney	$19.90

JEWELRY, HATPINS, WATCHES & PURSES

1712	Antique & Collector's **Thimbles** & Accessories, Mathis	$19.95
1748	Antique **Purses**, Revised Second Ed., Holiner	$19.95
1278	Art Nouveau & Art Deco **Jewelry**, Baker	$9.95
4558	Christmas Pins, Past and Present, Gallina	$18.95
3875	Collecting Antique **Stickpins**, Kerins	$16.95
3722	Collector's Ency. of **Compacts, Carryalls & Face Powder Boxes**, Mueller	$24.95
3992	Complete Price Guide to **Watches**, #15, Shugart	$21.95
1716	Fifty Years of Collector's **Fashion Jewelry**, 1925-1975, Baker	$19.95
1424	**Hatpins** & Hatpin Holders, Baker	$9.95
4570	Ladie's **Compacts**, Gerson	$24.95
1181	100 Years of Collectible **Jewelry**, Baker	$9.95
2348	20th Century Fashionable Plastic **Jewelry**, Baker	$19.95
3830	Vintage **Vanity Bags & Purses**, Gerson	$24.95

TOYS, MARBLES & CHRISTMAS COLLECTIBLES

3427	**Advertising Character** Collectibles, Dotz	$17.95
2333	Antique & Collector's **Marbles**, 3rd Ed., Grist	$9.95
3827	Antique & Collector's **Toys**, 1870–1950, Longest	$24.95
3956	Baby Boomer **Games**, Identification & Value Guide, Polizzi	$24.95

3717	**Christmas** Collectibles, 2nd Edition, Whitmyer	$24.95
1752	**Christmas** Ornaments, Lights & Decorations, Johnson	$19.95
3874	Collectible Coca-Cola Toy **Trucks**, deCourtivron	$24.95
2338	Collector's Encyclopedia of **Disneyana**, Longest, Stern	$24.95
2151	Collector's Guide to **Tootsietoys**, 2nd Ed., Richter	$16.95
3436	Grist's Big Book of **Marbles**	$19.95
3970	Grist's Machine-Made & Contemporary **Marbles**, 2nd Ed.	$9.95
3732	**Matchbox®** Toys, 1948 to 1993, Johnson	$18.95
3823	**Mego** Toys, An Illustrated Value Guide, Chrouch	15.95
1540	**Modern Toys** 1930–1980, Baker	$19.95
3888	**Motorcycle** Toys, Antique & Contemporary, Gentry/Downs	$18.95
3891	Schroeder's Collectible **Toys**, Antique to Modern Price Guide, 2nd Ed.	$17.95
1886	Stern's Guide to **Disney** Collectibles	$14.95
2139	Stern's Guide to **Disney** Collectibles, 2nd Series	$14.95
3975	Stern's Guide to **Disney** Collectibles, 3rd Series	$18.95
2028	**Toys**, Antique & Collectible, Longest	$14.95
3975	**Zany Characters** of the Ad World, Lamphier	$16.95

INDIANS, GUNS, KNIVES, TOOLS, PRIMITIVES

1868	Antique **Tools**, Our American Heritage, McNerney	$9.95
2015	Archaic **Indian** Points & Knives, Edler	$14.95
1426	**Arrowheads** & Projectile Points, Hothem	$7.95
2279	**Indian** Artifacts of the Midwest, Hothem	$14.95
3885	**Indian** Artifacts of the Midwest, Book II, Hothem	$16.95
1964	**Indian** Axes & Related Stone Artifacts, Hothem	$14.95
2023	**Keen Kutter** Collectibles, Heuring	$14.95
3887	Modern **Guns**, Identification & Values, 10th Ed., Quertermous	$12.95
4505	Standard Guide to **Razors**, Ritchie & Stewart	$9.95
3325	Standard **Knife** Collector's Guide, 2nd Ed., Ritchie & Stewart	$12.95

PAPER COLLECTIBLES & BOOKS

1441	Collector's Guide to **Post Cards**, Wood	$9.95
2081	Guide to Collecting **Cookbooks**, Allen	$14.95
3969	Huxford's **Old Book** Value Guide, 7th Ed.	$19.95
3821	Huxford's **Paperback** Value Guide	$19.95
2080	Price Guide to **Cookbooks & Recipe Leaflets**, Dickinson	$9.95
2346	**Sheet Music** Reference & Price Guide, 2nd Ed., Pafik & Guiheen	$18.95

GLASSWARE

1006	**Cambridge Glass** Reprint 1930–1934	$14.95
1007	**Cambridge Glass** Reprint 1949–1953	$14.95
2310	**Children's Glass Dishes, China & Furniture**, Vol. I, Lechler	$19.95
1627	**Children's Glass Dishes, China & Furniture**, Vol. II, Lechler	$19.95
4561	Collectible **Drinking Glasses**, Chase & Kelly	$17.95
3719	Coll. **Glassware** from the 40's, 50's & 60's, 3rd Ed., Florence	$19.95
2352	Collector's Encyclopedia of **Akro Agate Glassware**, Florence	$14.95
1810	Collector's Encyclopedia of **American Art Glass**, Shuman	$29.95
3312	Collector's Encyclopedia of **Children's Dishes**, Whitmyer	$19.95
3724	Collector's Encyclopedia of **Depression Glass**, 12th Ed., Florence	$19.95
1664	Collector's Encyclopedia of **Heisey Glass**, 1925–1938, Bredehoft	$24.95
3905	Collector's Encyclopedia of **Milk Glass**, Newbound	$24.95
1523	Colors In **Cambridge Glass**, National Cambridge Soceity	$19.95
4564	**Crackle Glass**, Weitman	$18.95
2275	**Czechoslovakian Glass** and Collectibles, Barta	$16.95
3882	**Elegant Glassware** of the Depression Era, 6th Ed., Florence	$19.95
1380	Encyclopedia of **Pattern Glass**, McClain	$12.95
3981	Ever's Standard **Cut Glass** Value Guide	$12.95
3725	**Fostoria**, Pressed, Blown & Hand Molded Shapes, Kerr	$24.95
3883	**Fostoria Stemware**, The Crystal for America, Long & Seate	$24.95
3318	**Glass Animals** of the Depression Era, Garmon & Spencer	$19.95
3886	**Kitchen Glassware** of the Depression Years, 5th Ed., Florence	$19.95
2394	**Oil Lamps II**, Glass Kerosene Lamps, Thuro	$24.95
3889	Pocket Guide to **Depression Glass**, 9th Ed., Florence	$9.95
3739	Standard Encyclopedia of **Carnival Glass**, 4th Ed., Edwards	$24.95

COLLECTOR BOOKS
Informing Today's Collector

BOOKS ON COLLECTIBLES

(Continued)

3740	Standard **Carnival Glass** Price Guide, 9th Ed.	$9.95
3974	Standard Encyclopedia of **Opalescent Glass**, Edwards	$19.95
1848	**Very Rare Glassware** of the Depression Years, Florence	$24.95
2140	**Very Rare Glassware** of the Depression Years, 2nd Series, Florence	$24.95
3326	**Very Rare Glassware** of the Depression Years, 3rd Series, Florence	$24.95
3909	**Very Rare Glassware** of the Depression Years, 4th Series, Florence	$24.95
2224	World of **Salt Shakers**, 2nd Ed., Lechner	$24.95

POTTERY

1312	**Blue & White Stoneware**, McNerney	$9.95
1958	So. Potteries **Blue Ridge Dinnerware**, 3rd Ed., Newbound	$14.95
1959	**Blue Willow**, 2nd Ed., Gaston	$14.95
3816	Collectible **Vernon Kilns**, Nelson	$24.95
3311	Collecting **Yellow Ware** – Id. & Value Guide, McAllister	$16.95
1373	Collector's Encyclopedia of **American Dinnerware**, Cunningham	$24.95
3815	Collector's Encyclopedia of **Blue Ridge Dinnerware**, Newbound	$19.95
2272	Collector's Encyclopedia of **California Pottery**, Chipman	$24.95
3811	Collector's Encyclopedia of **Colorado Pottery**, Carlton	$24.95
2133	Collector's Encyclopedia of **Cookie Jars**, Roerig	$24.95
3723	Collector's Encyclopedia of **Cookie Jars**, Volume II, Roerig	$24.95
3429	Collector's Encyclopedia of **Cowan Pottery**, Saloff	$24.95
2209	Collector's Encyclopedia of **Fiesta**, 7th Ed., Huxford	$19.95
3961	Collector's Encyclopedia of **Early Noritake**, Alden	$24.95
1439	Collector's Encyclopedia of **Flow Blue China**, Gaston	$19.95
3812	Collector's Encyclopedia of **Flow Blue China**, 2nd Ed., Gaston	$24.95
3813	Collector's Encyclopedia of **Hall China**, 2nd Ed., Whitmyer	$24.95
3431	Collector's Encyclopedia of **Homer Laughlin China**, Jasper	$24.95
1276	Collector's Encyclopedia of **Hull Pottery**, Roberts	$19.95
4573	Collector's Encyclopedia of **Knowles, Taylor & Knowles**, Gaston	$24.95
3962	Collector's Encyclopedia of **Lefton China**, DeLozier	$19.95
2210	Collector's Encyclopedia of **Limoges Porcelain**, 2nd Ed., Gaston	$24.95
2334	Collector's Encyclopedia of **Majolica Pottery**, Katz-Marks	$19.95
1358	Collector's Encyclopedia of **McCoy Pottery**, Huxford	$19.95
3963	Collector's Encyclopedia of **Metlox Potteries**, Gibbs Jr.	$24.95
3313	Collector's Encyclopedia of **Niloak**, Gifford	$19.95
3837	Collector's Encyclopedia of **Nippon Porcelain I**, Van Patten	$24.95
2089	Collector's Ency. of **Nippon Porcelain**, 2nd Series, Van Patten	$24.95
1665	Collector's Ency. of **Nippon Porcelain**, 3rd Series, Van Patten	$24.95
3836	**Nippon Porcelain** Price Guide, Van Patten	$9.95
1447	Collector's Encyclopedia of **Noritake**, Van Patten	$19.95
3432	Collector's Encyclopedia of **Noritake**, 2nd Series, Van Patten	$24.95
1037	Collector's Encyclopedia of **Occupied Japan**, Vol. I, Florence	$14.95
1038	Collector's Encyclopedia of **Occupied Japan**, Vol. II, Florence	$14.95
2088	Collector's Encyclopedia of **Occupied Japan**, Vol. III, Florence	$14.95
2019	Collector's Encyclopedia of **Occupied Japan**, Vol. IV, Florence	$14.95
2335	Collector's Encyclopedia of **Occupied Japan**, Vol. V, Florence	$14.95
3964	Collector's Encyclopedia of **Pickard China**, Reed	$24.95
1311	Collector's Encyclopedia of **R.S. Prussia**, 1st Series, Gaston	$24.95
1715	Collector's Encyclopedia of **R.S. Prussia**, 2nd Series, Gaston	$24.95
3726	Collector's Encyclopedia of **R.S. Prussia**, 3rd Series, Gaston	$24.95
3877	Collector's Encyclopedia of **R.S. Prussia**, 4th Series, Gaston	$24.95
1034	Collector's Encyclopedia of **Roseville Pottery**, Huxford	$19.95
1035	Collector's Encyclopedia of **Roseville Pottery**, 2nd Ed., Huxford	$19.95
3357	**Roseville** Price Guide No. 10	$9.95
2083	Collector's Encyclopedia of **Russel Wright** Designs, Kerr	$19.95
3965	Collector's Encyclopedia of **Sascha Brastoff**, Conti, Bethany & Seay	$24.95
3314	Collector's Encyclopedia of **Van Briggle** Art Pottery, Sasicki	$24.95
2111	Collector's Encyclopedia of **Weller Pottery**, Huxford	$29.95
3452	Coll. Guide to Country Stoneware & Pottery, Raycraft	$11.95
2077	Coll. Guide to **Country Stoneware & Pottery**, 2nd Series, Raycraft	$14.95
3433	Collector's Guide To **Harker Pottery** - U.S.A., Colbert	$17.95
3434	Coll. Guide to **Hull Pottery**, The Dinnerware Line, Gick-Burke	$16.95

3876	Collector's Guide to **Lu-Ray Pastels**, Meehan	$18.95
3814	Collector's Guide to **Made in Japan** Ceramics, White	$18.95
4565	Collector's Guide to **Rockingham**, The Enduring Ware, Brewer	$14.95
2339	Collector's Guide to **Shawnee Pottery**, Vanderbilt	$19.95
1425	**Cookie Jars**, Westfall	$9.95
3440	**Cookie Jars**, Book II, Westfall	$19.95
3435	Debolt's Dictionary of **American Pottery Marks**	$17.95
2379	Lehner's Ency. of **U.S. Marks** on Pottery, Porcelain & China	$24.95
3825	**Puritan Pottery**, Morris	$24.95
1670	**Red Wing Collectibles**, DePasquale	$9.95
1440	**Red Wing Stoneware**, DePasquale	$9.95
3738	**Shawnee Pottery**, Mangus	$24.95
3327	**Watt Pottery** – Identification & Value Guide, Morris	$19.95

OTHER COLLECTIBLES

2269	Antique **Brass & Copper** Collectibles, Gaston	$16.95
1880	Antique **Iron**, McNerney	$9.95
3872	Antique **Tins**, Dodge	$24.95
1714	**Black** Collectibles, Gibbs	$19.95
1128	**Bottle** Pricing Guide, 3rd Ed., Cleveland	$7.95
3959	**Cereal Box** Bonanza, The 1950's, Bruce	$19.95
3718	Collectible **Aluminum**, Grist	$16.95
3445	Collectible **Cats**, An Identification & Value Guide, Fyke	$18.95
4560	Collectible **Cats**, An Identification & Value Guide, Book II, Fyke	$19.95
4563	Collector's Encyclopedia of **Wall Pockets**, Newbound	$19.95
1634	Collector's Ency. of Figural & Novelty **Salt & Pepper Shakers**, Davern	$19.95
2020	Collector's Ency. of Figural & Novelty **Salt & Pepper Shakers**, Vol. II, Davern	$19.95
2018	Collector's Encyclopedia of **Granite Ware**, Greguire	$24.95
3430	Collector's Encyclopedia of **Granite Ware**, Book II, Greguire	$24.95
3879	Collector's Guide to **Antique Radios**, 3rd Ed., Bunis	$18.95
1916	Collector's Guide to **Art Deco**, Gaston	$14.95
3880	Collector's Guide to **Cigarette Lighters**, Flanagan	$17.95
1537	Collector's Guide to **Country Baskets**, Raycraft	$9.95
3966	Collector's Guide to **Inkwells**, Identification & Values, Badders	$18.95
3881	Collector's Guide to **Novelty Radios**, Bunis/Breed	$18.95
3729	Collector's Guide to **Snow Domes**, Guarnaccia	$18.95
3730	Collector's Guide to **Transistor Radios**, Bunis	$15.95
2276	**Decoys**, Kangas	$24.95
1629	**Doorstops**, Identification & Values, Bertoia	$9.95
4567	Figural **Napkin Rings**, Gottschalk & Whitson	$18.95
3968	**Fishing Lure** Collectibles, Murphy/Edmisten	$24.95
3817	**Flea Market Trader**, 10th Ed., Huxford	$12.95
3976	Foremost Guide to **Uncle Sam** Collectibles, Czulewicz	$24.95
3819	**General Store** Collectibles, Wilson	$24.95
2215	Goldstein's **Coca-Cola** Collectibles	$16.95
3884	Huxford's Collectible **Advertising**, 2nd Ed.	$24.95
2216	**Kitchen Antiques**, 1790–1940, McNerney	$14.95
3321	Ornamental & Figural **Nutcrackers**, Rittenhouse	$16.95
2026	**Railroad** Collectibles, 4th Ed., Baker	$14.95
1632	**Salt & Pepper Shakers**, Guarnaccia	$9.95
1888	**Salt & Pepper Shakers** II, Identification & Value Guide, Book II, Guarnaccia	$14.95
2220	**Salt & Pepper Shakers** III, Guarnaccia	$14.95
3443	**Salt & Pepper Shakers** IV, Guarnaccia	$18.95
4555	**Schroeder's Antiques** Price Guide, 14th Ed., Huxford	$14.95
2096	**Silverplated Flatware**, Revised 4th Edition, Hagan	$14.95
1922	Standard **Old Bottle** Price Guide, Sellari	$14.95
3892	**Toy & Miniature Sewing Machines**, Thomas	$18.95
3828	Value Guide to **Advertising Memorabilia**, Summers	$18.95
3977	Value Guide to **Gas Station** Memorabilia, Summers & Priddy	$24.95
4572	**Wall Pockets** of the Past, Perkins	$17.95
3444	**Wanted to Buy**, 5th Edition	$9.95